Motivating
Black Males
to Achieve
IN SCHOOL & IN LIFE

Motivating Black Males to Achieve

BARUTI K. KAFELE

Alexandria, Virginia USA

1703 N. Beauregard St. • Alexandria, VA 22311 1714 USA
Phone: 800-933-2723 or 703-578-9600 • Fax: 703-575-5400
Web site: www.ascd.org • E-mail: member@ascd.org
Author guidelines: www.ascd.org/write

Gene R. Carter, *Executive Director;* Nancy Modrak, *Publisher;* Scott Willis, *Director, Book Acquisitions & Development;* Julie Houtz, *Director, Book Editing & Production;* Ernesto Yermoli, *Associate Editor;* Judi Connelly, *Senior Graphic Designer;* Mike Kalyan, *Production Manager;* Cynthia Stock, *Typesetter;* Sarah Plumb, *Production Specialist*

Printed in the United States of America. Cover art copyright © 2009 by ASCD. ASCD publications present a variety of viewpoints. The views expressed or implied in this book should not be interpreted as official positions of the Association.

All Web links in this book are correct as of the publication date below but may have become inactive or otherwise modified since that time. If you notice a deactivated or changed link, please e-mail books@ascd.org with the words "Link Update" in the subject line. In your message, please specify the Web link, the book title, and the page number on which the link appears.

ASCD Member Book, No. FY09-9 (Aug. 2009, P). ASCD Member Books mail to Premium (P), Select (S), and Institutional Plus (I+) members on this schedule: Jan., PSI+; Feb., P; Apr., PSI+; May, P; July, PSI+; Aug., P; Sept., PSI+; Nov., PSI+; Dec., P. Select membership was formerly known as Comprehensive membership.

PAPERBACK ISBN: 978-1-4166-0857-8   ASCD product #109013
Also available as an e-book (see Books in Print for the ISBNs).

Quantity discounts for the paperback edition only: 10–49 copies, 10%; 50+ copies, 15%; for 1,000 or more copies, call 800-933-2723, ext. 5634, or 703-575-5634. For desk copies: member@ascd.org.

Library of Congress Cataloging-in-Publication Data

Kafele, Baruti K.
  Motivating Black males to achieve in school and in life / Baruti K. Kafele.
      p. cm.
  Includes bibliographical references and index.
  ISBN 978-1-4166-0857-8 (pbk. : alk. paper) 1. African American young men—Education. 2. African American men—Education. 3. African American boys—Social conditions. 4. African American young men—Social conditions. 5. Academic achievement—United States. I. Title.
  LC2731.K34 2009
  371.829'96073—dc22

                                                                                          2009021025

20 19 18 17 16 15 14 13 12 11 10 09   1 2 3 4 5 6 7 8 9 10 11 12

This book is dedicated to all educators of black males.

Your black males' educational success rests largely on your shoulders.

I am confident that this book will help your students to

maximize their potential in school and beyond.

Motivating
Black Males
to Achieve
IN SCHOOL & IN LIFE

ACKNOWLEDGMENTS

In my previous books, I thanked all of the people who influenced my growth and development as an educator, an orator, and a man, including the students and staff in the schools that I served as principal. Since my last book was published, I have been the principal of Newark Tech High School in Newark, New Jersey. These past four years have been the most fulfilling of my career; the strides we have made in such a short period of time are attributable to the extraordinary students and staff at Newark Tech. In four short years, we were collectively able to demonstrate to the world what inner-city black and Latino children can do academically, socially, and emotionally when they are surrounded with dedicated educators and support staff. As the focus of this book is on motivating black males, I should note that I am particularly pleased with what our black males have accomplished over the years. I, too, have grown tremendously as a principal. To that end, I want to take this opportunity to publicly thank my entire Newark Tech family for a job well done!

To my Patrick Healy family of students, staff, and parents in East Orange, New Jersey: Thank you for getting me through "the storm of 2004"—especially my parent coordinator, Ms. Delores Wallace.

To the Open Line Crew at 98.7 KISS FM in New York City—Bob Slade, James Mtume, Bob Pickett, and Fatiyn Muhammad: Thank you immensely for always being in my corner.

To the parents and community of New Jersey and New York City: Thank you for all of the support and encouragement you have given me over the years.

To my Corinthian Baptist Church family in Jersey City, under the leadership of Pastor Damon Gilyard: Thank you for your continuous support and encouragement.

To Scott Willis of ASCD: Thank you for seeing in my work a potential book, and for staying on my case to write one since we first discussed it at the 2005 ASCD Conference.

To my editor, Ernesto Yermoli: Thank you for helping shape my thoughts into an excellent book of which I am most proud.

And of course, To my wife of 20 years, Kimberley; my children, Baruti, Jabari, and Kibriya; my mother, Delores Cushnie; and my father, Norman Hopkins: Thank you for your undying support of all of my endeavors—including my newest venture of pursuing a private pilot's license so that I can continue to soar!

PREFACE

Since entering the field of education in 1988 as a 5th grade teacher in Brooklyn, New York, I have worked predominantly with black students. In my capacities as a classroom teacher, a vice principal, and a principal, my intention has always been to increase the probability for student success.

As a classroom teacher in an urban school district in New Jersey, where I spent the bulk of my career (or my "mission," as I refer to it), I consistently felt that my students could and would achieve academic excellence under my guidance. My attitude was that my students would be successful because I was their teacher. I worked quite hard with these youngsters over the years, understanding full well that if I was going to be an effective teacher, I had to keep my students motivated and inspired about learning. If I could do that, then learning would certainly follow.

Much of my success in keeping my students motivated and inspired was due to the passion, energy, and enthusiasm that I brought to my lessons all day, every day. I knew that if my delivery was boring, I was going to have a hard time keeping students not only motivated, but focused as well. I wanted my students to be just as excited about learning as I was about teaching. If you teach black males, then you must consistently strive to bring a passion, energy, and enthusiasm to your lessons, regardless of the subject. If you are boring, your students will be bored.

When I became a vice principal, I once again understood that if I was going to be a successful administrator, I had to keep students motivated, inspired, and focused. One of the first things I did was to transform the appearance of the school: I posted positive affirmation signs all over the school's hallways, stairwells, and cafeteria. These areas of the school became, in a sense, my own personal classroom. I encouraged the students to read these signs daily as they walked from class to class. Between classes, I'd bring students to any given sign and commence teaching on the topic of the affirmation. I also put up posters of noteworthy black historical figures all over the school, because I wanted my students not only to be exposed to positive messages, but also to positive images. I was essentially creating a positive school atmosphere—a necessary first step toward ensuring student academic success. When I became a principal, I once again transformed the building by posting positive affirmations and images, and also focused on the quality of teacher-student interactions in each and every classroom.

In each of my capacities as teacher, vice principal, and principal, the end result of my efforts was the same: my students' scores consistently improved, both on report cards and on standardized tests. These successes inspired me to write and speak to a broader audience, which I eventually did, at the ASCD National Conference of 2004.

The conference was to take place in New Orleans, at the downtown convention center. I was assigned a 300-seat room on a Monday afternoon. I arrived on Thursday so that I could also partake of some of the other sessions for my own professional growth. As Monday drew closer and closer, my anxiety rose. Each day, at least twice per day, I would walk to my assigned room and look at all of the seats. I envisioned them full of educators, listening to me share my strategies for successfully educating black students. However, I also began to wonder what I would do if no one showed up, or if the turnout was minimal. How would I get my message across if no one bothered to attend my session?

Well, on the morning of my session, the educators came. It was unbelievable! The room was packed to capacity; many had to be turned away. I felt on fire and ready to deliver. When my session concluded, I received a huge ovation. This reaction affirmed that the audience found my presentation beneficial. At least half of the attendees approached me afterward. Some just wanted to say thanks; others had questions. Many wanted strategies for motivating and meeting the classroom needs of black male students in particular. Being at a national conference had given me an opportunity to hear the concerns and frustrations of teachers from all over the country.

The reaction of my audience made me realize that the plight of black males is a larger concern for educators nationally than I had previously thought. I therefore decided that I would conduct more research in this area and run professional development workshops devoted to educators of black males. In the past few years I have done just that.

So many educators, however well intentioned, are simply at a loss for what to do to improve the performance of their black male students. I receive an enormous number of e-mails from educators at all levels asking for solutions to the myriad of challenges that they face with their black males. No matter which part of the country you go to, the problems are quite similar. I have had men and women approach me in tears about some of the young black males in their classroom, exasperated at the behavioral or academic challenge that these students often pose. They expressed that their students lacked motivation or even the desire to be in school at all. It's not the students' fault, however: Each individual student has his own unique set of needs, which requires that his teacher understand him personally and the need for differentiation generally. Even a brilliant student needs a teacher who understands how to make solid connections with him.

When teachers voice their frustrations about particular students, I often desperately wish I could actually meet the young men in question and encourage them to reach for the highest of heights. Of course, these young men can be found in practically every school across the country. They come to class every day full of potential for excellence, but they also have needs that must be met by their teachers. They require teachers who are equipped with the necessary knowledge and skills to make solid and meaningful connections with them. They don't mean any harm; they desire success just like anyone else, but may have different requirements than some of their peers. If these students are going to meet their potential for success, then teachers must meet their unique needs. Doing so will essentially level the playing field so that young black males have a fair chance of competing with everyone else.

My purpose for writing this book is to provide educators with a practical blueprint for meeting the classroom needs of black male students. Do understand, however, that this book is not meant to be a quick fix; there are no quick fixes for meeting the needs of black males. Rather, meeting classroom needs requires a sustained process, with the teacher remaining consistent throughout. Teachers must never become so discouraged that they concede defeat. The plight of black males did not occur overnight, and neither will its solution. It is going to take time, but it is vital that the actual problems are being addressed.

Lack of proficiency in reading, writing, and math among black males is a symptom of deeper problems that have gone ignored, unaddressed, and unmet for far too long. Throughout this book, I will identify these problems and offer solutions that teachers can implement in their daily practice.

All children can learn—I strongly believe this. But before learning can occur, all children must be motivated, whether intrinsically or extrinsically, to *want* to learn. When this happens, the dream of large numbers of black males joining the honor roll and receiving academic scholarships can finally become reality.

Of course, unless you teach at a school with only black male students, you will face the challenge of applying the strategies contained in this book while simultaneously teaching all of the other types of learners in your classroom. Although differentiation of this sort is an additional challenge to an already challenging endeavor, it is not only doable, it is unavoidable. Although many of the strategies in this book are easily applicable to different types of students, my focus is on black males, as their plight continues to be the greatest challenge for teachers across the country.

INTRODUCTION

Black males compose a little over 6 percent of the total U.S. population (McKinnon & Bennett, 2005). Literally millions of black males have achieved great things with their lives despite the challenges they've faced. Unfortunately, the media tend to focus on the minority of black men who have gotten into trouble with the law (for example) rather than the majority who are doing significant things with their lives and in their communities. My travels and experiences have demonstrated to me that black male success stories are far more common than many people may believe. These are the stories that must be sought out and told as frequently as possible to serve as examples for others.

As a public elementary school student in an urban school district in northern New Jersey in the late 1960s, I had few academic and social problems. I was an average student, not quite working to my potential, but nevertheless achieving the occasional As and Bs. I liked school, I liked my teachers, and I looked forward to going to school every day; I felt that it was a fun and worthwhile experience. I lived at home with my mother and maternal grandmother, but had an ongoing relationship with my father as well. All of my friends lived on my block, and all of our parents held us accountable for proper conduct while outside. Everyone in the neighborhood knew everyone else, which helped ensure that all of us did the right thing at all times.

When I entered high school, I was not prepared for the social dynamic that I encountered. As a young, inner-city black male, I felt enormous pressure to comply with the expected code of conduct for young black men as defined by my peers. Academic success became secondary and ultimately unimportant. My drive to succeed deteriorated to such a degree that my mother decided to move us to the suburbs, away from the distractions of the city.

This transition was a true culture shock. Instead of being part of the majority population, I was now instantly in the miniscule minority: I was one of only five black students in a high school of around 2,000. I learned very quickly that people in my new surroundings held certain assumptions. For example, because I was a tall black male, many of my peers thought that I had superior skills in basketball. Although I could hold my own and compete, I was by no means exceptional.

As a student, I unfortunately did not hold my own. I was not the student that I had the potential of becoming. Looking back on my experience now, it's clear that I never sensed any high expectation for me to be successful. Although I am aware that I had good teachers in elementary and high school, I cannot think of one who made a difference for me—one who met my classroom needs and inspired me to strive for excellence. My teachers didn't challenge me to excel academically, so I spent most of my energy on trying to adapt to my new environment and enhance my basketball skills. By comparison, my academic progress was of little importance. I did ultimately graduate, but I had to make up a lot of what I missed in junior college.

Finally, in college, I achieved academic excellence, ultimately graduating *summa cum laude.* This did not happen by chance, however: My public-speaking professor uttered three words to me that "turned on the light bulb," and I haven't looked back ever since. I had never given a speech before taking his class, and the prospect of doing so in front of my peers terrified me; being one of the few black students in the class only made matters worse. When it came time for me to give a speech, I told the professor that I couldn't do it. He told me that I had to, so I somehow found the courage to present one. When I was done, the professor said to me, "You speak well."

I had never heard this before. I was not aware of my potential as a public speaker, and therefore had not previously desired to speak publicly. As a result of what the professor said, I have been speaking publicly ever since.

The professor told me something about myself that I did not know. He inspired me, and as a result, I have been striving to be the best speaker that I can possibly be ever since he uttered those three words. To this day, I have no idea as to whether or not he was sincere, but that's not important. What *is* important is that I believed what he said and acted upon it. I believed that he saw something in me that I did not see in myself and took the time to let me know. Those three words that he uttered to me are what I credit for my success as a speaker over the past 22 years.

I was inspired anew when I entered graduate school. One of the courses I took required a great deal of writing. Once again, I was one of the few black male students in the class. When the professor handed back the first paper I had written—not only the first paper for the class, but the first I had written on the graduate level—he said to me, "You write well." Once again, I received three life-changing words from a significant figure. I initially expressed disbelief, but he insisted that I was a good writer. I had never heard this before; I did not know that I had any writing skills worth mentioning. Since hearing those three important words, I have gone on to write five books.

I once again heard three life-changing words in one of my leadership courses. One day, in front of the entire class, the professor said to me, "You're a leader." He didn't stop there, however. He proceeded to say, "You're not just an ordinary leader—you are a *transformational* leader." Until that point in my life, I had never really viewed myself as a leader. I was still an elementary school teacher when I was taking the leadership course, but the professor sensed that my leadership qualities could help transform the school and possibly the district in which I worked. To this day, my leadership approach has been transformational. I am never satisfied with the status quo; I am always looking for ways to transform existing structures for the betterment of my students.

Teachers of black males have a responsibility to inspire them the way my professors inspired me. In my capacity as a principal, I announce to my students over the public address system every day that they are "most brilliant and most highly capable." I remind them that they are born with the potential to achieve excellence and greatness. I frequently say to educators that our roles are to motivate, educate, and empower—in that order. When we choose our words wisely and consider the power that words can have, we increase the probability that our students will achieve excellence. We must always remain mindful of the power and influence that we possess as educators, and we must use every opportunity that we have throughout the day to make our students aware of their greatness. If we fail to do this, the streets have a way of picking up the slack.

As you read this book, you'll notice that I ask a plethora of questions. I do this in an effort to get you to think deeply about what you are already doing and what adjustments you may need to make to your current practice. You will quickly find that you already possess the answers to many of the questions you have about meeting the classroom needs of black male students.

CHAPTER 1

Learning About
Black Male Students
to Meet Their
Classroom Needs

It is said that you cannot teach what you do not know. I couldn't agree more. Imagine that you are a 6th grade language arts teacher with no background in science, and your principal asks you to teach two periods of science every day. How are you going to be effective? How are you going to be enthusiastic? How are you going to hold the attention of your students? It is going to be very difficult, if not impossible, under these circumstances.

Now, imagine that you are teaching the content area that you have been trained to teach, but you know nothing about your students. Let's say that you have a sizable number of black males in your class. What do you know about this specific population of students? Are you prepared to connect with them? Do you know not only how to motivate them, but how to keep them motivated over a long period? Do you know what their classroom needs are? Are you prepared to address and meet their classroom needs? Unless you can answer these questions, your students' success (and, therefore, your success as a teacher) would be very difficult to achieve. Ask yourself what you know about your black male students'

- Need for inspiration;
- Learning styles;
- Goals and aspirations;
- Experiences and realities;
- Needs and interests;
- Challenges, obstacles, and distractions;
- Peers, parents, and neighborhoods; and
- History and culture.

Do you know enough about all these issues? Let's explore each one individually.

Need for Inspiration

One of my favorite educational quotes is from William Arthur Ward:

> *Mediocre teachers tell.*
> *Good teachers explain.*
> *Superior teachers demonstrate.*
> *Great teachers inspire.*

One of the first steps toward becoming a great, inspiring teacher is to concentrate on building strong relationships with your students while simultaneously making learning fun (Kunjufu, 2002). As obvious and rudimentary as it may sound, your students must actually *like* you if they are to do well in class—and in order for them to like you, you must show that *you* like *them*. In an ideal situation, you would demonstrate that you loved them, cared about them, and appreciated them without ever having to say it. Students should be able to sense how you feel about them through your words and your actions. Trust me, if you do not like them or do not want to be bothered with them, they will know how you feel through what you say to them and how you say it.

If you build a solid relationship with your students, they will expect you to consistently treat them respectfully and fairly, as equals. You must be able to demonstrate to them that you are genuinely interested in them and their overall growth and well-being beyond their academic progress. They want and need to know that you are interested in them as individuals. Many of them simply want someone to listen to their concerns and offer suggestions. You can help meet these needs by interacting with students in the cafeteria, in the hallways, on the playground, outside before and after school, or in class before and after the bell rings. As their teacher, you are a significant person in your students' lives. You have the power to mold your students into successful high achievers, but you must first build solid relationships with them.

There is much about your own life that can serve as a source of inspiration for your students. All of us have our own unique experiences that led to our individual accomplishments, but until we have earned our students' trust, our stories will probably be unimportant and uninspiring to them. I have seen many educators try to share their experiences with students when they had not yet earned their trust. Needless to say, these educators' words went in one ear and out the other.

You must always keep at the forefront of your mind that you are a teacher of students first, and of subjects second. The human factor must always be the first priority. It is so much easier for students to learn from those they know, like, and trust than from those with whom they have no relationship.

In addition to building solid relationships with your students, you must also ensure that learning is stimulating, engaging, and, most important, fun. For example, black males struggle with mathematics more than any other subject. In each of the four schools where I have been principal, I have paid particular attention to what goes on in the math classes. After analyzing which math teachers are more successful than others with black males, the reason for their success becomes obvious: they build solid relationships with their students and are committed to making learning fun. Their classroom environments and lessons are student-centered, and boredom is nowhere to be found. The teachers understand that with each lesson, they must bring a high degree of energy, enthusiasm, and passion to their students to keep them consistently inspired about learning.

In addition to being inspired to *learn,* your black males must also be motivated to *excel.* Do you possess effective strategies for keeping your black male students motivated? Do you know what they require to stay motivated? If your students are unmotivated, do you know why? How have you addressed their lack of motivation? Ask yourself if their lack of motivation has anything to do with the following:

- Your instructional methodology
- Lack of individuality in your instruction
- The level of difficulty of your instruction
- Lack of interest in your content area
- Lack of prior understanding in your content area
- Low reading comprehension skills
- Your relationship with your students
- Your classroom seating arrangement
- The other students in the classroom
- Peer pressure
- The students' home life
- Neighborhood issues
- Other priorities

You must be willing to make whatever adjustments are necessary in your classroom for your students to be motivated to excel. If there are home or neighborhood issues, you will need to investigate, along with other school stakeholders, to ascertain what the school can do to help resolve the issues.

Bear in mind that in order for your students to be motivated to excel, your students must first have goals. They should be required to set goals for each marking period and post them on the wall, and to write down their strategies for achieving each goal. Once goals have been set, you must seek any possible excuse to celebrate when students achieve them: selecting students of the week/month, recognizing homework submission, posting student work samples regularly, and recognizing perfect attendance are just a few of the ways to do so. You must personally take every opportunity to make a big deal of your students' accomplishments. When they see that you are genuinely excited about their progress, they will be more likely to continue to strive for excellence. In my capacity as principal, in addition to the normal honor roll breakfast and certificates, I make sure that I shake hands with, hug, and congratulate as many of my honor roll students as I can when I see them in the hallways between classes. Of course, this requires that I know all of my students and study the names on the honor roll. Imagine the reaction of my black male students when I express sincere excitement about their achievements by shaking their hands and hugging them for everyone in the hallway to see. Trust me—it goes a long way.

Learning Styles

All children do not learn alike. Do you know how your black male students learn? Do they all learn alike? Do they learn in the same way as your black females or students of other ethnic groups? Does culture play a role? Do life experiences play a role? In order to achieve success with your black male students, these are questions that you must consider in your daily lesson preparation.

When I was in school, most of my teachers used the lecture format to deliver instruction. Lectures obviously appeal to auditory learners, but they are the worst instructional strategy to use with students who do not learn best simply by listening. I myself have never been an auditory learner, but my teachers never took my particular learning style into consideration. I am confident that if my teachers had determined the learning styles of their students and differentiated their instruction accordingly, we would have performed much better than we did.

At my own school, I remind my staff that just because they are excited about the lessons they have developed doesn't mean that their students are equally excited. I remind them that they must take into consideration the learning styles of all of the learners in their classrooms, including their black males. When teachers take the time to learn how their students learn, the probability for actual learning increases for all students in the classroom.

It is not easy to discern the different learning styles of your students. You must first get to know your students. In a teacher-centered learning environment where teachers do most of the talking, it is virtually impossible to adequately ascertain how the students learn, because the students are reduced to passive learning. The classroom learning environment must instead be student-centered, as this enables you to observe your students engaging in active learning. In a student-centered classroom, you get to watch your students participate in a variety of different learning activities that require them to use a variety of different problem-solving skills. These observations place you in a better position to reach informed conclusions about how your students learn.

Goals and Aspirations

What are the goals of your black male students? Do they have concrete academic goals? Do they want to be honor roll students? Do they want high GPAs? Is graduating with a high school diploma a high priority for them? What role have you played in helping them reach their goals? Teachers of black males must maintain the highest possible standards and expectations for them, whatever the challenges and obstacles.

Each spring, I am invited to speak at several inner-city graduations, which I consider to be an honor. The 8th grade graduations are my favorites: Parents are typically very excited, as though their kids were graduating from high school or college. At around the middle of all my graduation speeches, I have the male students stand to be recognized and applauded. The crowd typically gives these young men a thunderous ovation. I believe they do so because these young men need and require all of the praise that they can get. The odds are certainly against many of them: On the national level, the statistics say that only half of them will see another graduation (Schott Foundation for Public Education, 2008). Many parents are fully aware of the possibility that this graduation may be their son's last.

While the young men are standing, I passionately say to them: "This cannot be your final graduation. You must work diligently for the next four years so that you may graduate once again with your high school diploma. But it does not stop there: You must then proceed to college, which you planned for throughout your high school experience. But it does not stop there either: You must then proceed to earn your master's degree, and then your doctorate." By this time the parents and families are in a frenzy. They are giving the young men ovation after ovation. Some are even in tears. It becomes evident to me that the young men feel quite good about themselves for graduating.

We as educators must help our students to set goals and develop plans of action for reaching those goals, and we must hold students accountable for striving toward their goals throughout the years they are in school. Regardless of the grade level, the most important goal that students must set is that of going to college. Even at the elementary school level, black males must focus on ultimately attending college. I cringe whenever I hear an adult say that college is not for everyone. Even if this claim has any merit to it, grade school children must be exposed to teachers and other stakeholders who instill in them the value of a college education. Of course, students must have other goals as well. To know your students, you must familiarize yourself with these goals and help ensure that they are consistent with their educational growth and development.

You must also be familiar with your students' aspirations. It is far easier to motivate them when you know what it is that they aspire to become. What are the aspirations of your black males? What do they want to do with their lives beyond high school? How much of a commitment are they willing to invest in themselves? Are their aspirations being dictated by their belief in themselves, or by a lack thereof?

In talking with black male teenagers over the years, I have learned that far too many feel that they will not live to see life beyond the age 21. They feel that it would be useless for them to expend much energy on trying to fulfill their aspirations, because they will never live long enough to see them come true. Sadly, this is a national problem. Why do so many black male students think along these lines? Your role as a classroom teacher is to change this destructive thinking so that your black male students can see themselves as young men with limitless opportunities and possibilities.

Experiences and Realities

Not long ago, a black male 9th grader was sent to my office because he reported to class without a pencil. I was aware that he lived in a neighborhood where it was a challenge just to walk to school every day. The simple fact that he showed up on time to school was to be commended considering his circumstances. After meeting with the student, I asked the teacher if she realized what he had to endure every day just to get to school. She said that she did not. I told her that his pattern of timely attendance bordered on miraculous.

Regardless of their ethnicity, teachers who have never lived in the inner city could probably never imagine much less endure the hardships that many of their students face. Many black males have to walk past street gangs every day just to get to school in the morning. On the day that I write this, one of my 9th graders was jumped, assaulted, and robbed on his way to our freshman summer enrichment program. Many young black males also have to endure the pressure to join gangs; some even end up joining gangs simply to remain safe and keep the gangs off of their backs.

You must make an effort to stay aware of your students' everyday experiences. You must also be mindful that your students may not openly and voluntarily discuss these experiences with you unless you ask. Even if asked, chances are good that they may still not want to disclose any information unless you first build trust with your students.

As we all know, black males in the United States have been the victims of extreme racism for generations. Your black male students are the products of this long and difficult journey. They are the ones who carry the scars. It is imperative that you consider the consequences of racism that your students must endure, because it has a direct impact on their motivation to learn. Take racial profiling, for example. As a black man, despite my professional accomplishments and status, I continue to find myself in situations where I am treated as a suspected criminal for no other reason than my skin color. Many of the students in your classroom face the same reality in their neighborhoods. Because of the wrongs of a few, many of them find themselves being profiled and harassed by the police for doing nothing more than walking down the street to their homes from school or hanging out with friends. Their frustration about this fact has a direct bearing on their motivation to excel in the classroom.

Needs and Interests

As a teacher of black male students, there is a great deal that you are required to know about them. Like every other group, black males have their own unique set of needs. One of the most important for you to consider is the need for black males to be accepted by their peers. Many black males are more concerned with being accepted by their peers than with being smart. Even in the new millennium, there are still many black adolescents who perceive being smart as corny, nerdy, or "acting white." You must challenge this line of thinking by consistently encouraging your students to strive to be the brightest that they can possibly be.

In addition to having particular needs, black males also have certain interests that may affect motivation and learning, and which you therefore must ascertain. A couple of times in two different schools, I assigned my entire staff to spend a portion of their summer listening to hardcore, unedited hip hop music. I reminded my staff that many of our black males were not only listening to this music, but aspired to become hip hop artists themselves. Upon returning to school from summer break, many staff members expressed surprise at the extreme vulgarity of the lyrics and at the fact that so many youngsters had such easy access to them, but were able to more fully appreciate why the music was so appealing to their black male students.

Because so many black males identify strongly with hip hop music, teachers must be acutely familiar with its messages—particularly if these messages diminish the appeal of classroom learning. By developing a broader awareness of the music that many young black males listen to, educators are better able to counteract its negative aspects. I asked my staff to listen to hip hop because I wanted them to be able to discover for themselves the challenges that hip hop lyrics present for effective teaching and learning in the classroom. I wanted my teachers to understand that when young men internalize and take ownership of such lyrics, it becomes all the more challenging to connect with them.

Obviously, black males have other interests besides music. Do you know what some of these interests may be and how they affect motivation and learning?

Challenges, Obstacles, and Distractions

Teachers must be knowledgeable of the unique set of challenges that black males face. For example, it is a challenge for many black males to let their guard down and demonstrate to their teachers and peers how intelligent they truly are. As previously noted, it is not always cool to be smart among black males due to their perceived stereotypes of what it is to be a black male; if they attempt to demonstrate their intelligence, they may be ostracized or ridiculed by their peers. A related challenge that black males face is the myth that to be smart is to "act white" and therefore not be "down," "cool," or "black." The alternative then is to "act black," which in the eyes of too many black males is to forgo their natural intelligence at the expense of high academic achievement. As the classroom teacher, your job is to anticipate these challenges and to help students overcome them by changing their thinking and the overall culture of the classroom so that it becomes acceptable to be smart and intelligent.

Some challenges become obstacles that are never surmounted. For instance, when I give a speech, as an attention-grabber, I often tell my audience that I will be speaking to them in two languages: my primary language of ebonics and my secondary language of English. I let them know that I have mastered the former but still struggle with aspects of the latter. This typically results in reserved laughter from the audience, but the reality is that this is precisely the case with many black people. Black male students expect one another to be fluent in ebonics; if they are not, they are often accused of "speaking white." Speaking standard English can cause ridicule, thereby limiting the students' desire to practice it in the classroom.

There is a tremendous absence of positive black male role models in the lives of so many black boys. According to research data, almost 70 percent of black children are born into households where there is only one parent present, typically the mother (Parker, 2008). This means that these children are going home to households where there is no male figure or male role model present.

There is similarly an absence of black male teachers—particularly at the elementary level, where most teachers are white women. Black males can go through their entire school experience without having had one teacher who looked like them and to whom they could therefore relate. My oldest son, who just graduated from an urban high school in New Jersey, never had a single black male teacher. My other son, who is a sophomore in high school, had his first black male teacher for 8th grade science—one period per day. My sons are fortunate enough to have a committed father in their home who is well aware of his role model status. But what about the hundreds of thousands of others who do not?

The absence of positive black male role models in the lives of black boys essentially creates a distraction. Many of these boys will search for people who look like them for leadership, guidance, and direction in the wrong places—among "gang bangers" in the streets, in music, on television, or in movies. You must do what you can to bring attention to this problem and help students understand that they themselves will be looked up to one day. You must make them aware of the fact that throughout history, black men have played prominent roles and made significant accomplishments in all walks of life, well beyond the worlds of sports and entertainment.

Peers, Parents, and Neighborhoods

Peers

I have said to parents over the years that they can do all of the right things in terms of raising, nurturing, and educating their children just to have it all unravel when their children leave for school in the morning. Just as parents must be familiar with their children's peers, teachers must be as well. You must monitor closely the acquaintances with whom your black male students choose to surround themselves. If these individuals exhibit characteristics that are inconsistent with the positive values that you are attempting to instill, you will have to hold immediate and ongoing conversations with your students regarding the choices that that they are making. Of course, to be credible, your students must perceive you as trustworthy enough to intervene. As you anticipate and ascertain problems that they encounter, they will need you to help them get back on track, whether they know it or not. As I say to my students, "Your teachers are your best friends. Be sure to get all of the knowledge and wisdom from them that you can while you have them as your teachers."

Parents

Many educators complain about the lack of parental involvement in their students' educational lives. They complain that the parents do not participate enough at home and that their attendance at school meetings is minimal. This is a valid concern, and teachers must persist in encouraging parental participation. When I became a teacher, I learned this very early on. I couldn't believe the lack of parent involvement. I especially needed the parents to be involved in the lives of their sons, because I was witnessing too many males raising themselves, or being raised by poor models, on the streets. I therefore decided that if the parents were not going to be involved at the level that I felt that they could and should be involved, I was going to knock on their doors. I not only wanted the parents to be involved, but I wanted to get to know them and gauge my students' home lives. At least three afternoons per week, I would visit students at their homes. This enabled me to get to know their parents, and them to get to know me. Moreover, it allowed me to convey to the parents what I expected of them in terms of reinforcing my lessons at home. I found these visits to be extremely helpful, especially for my male students. I found that most of them had no fathers at home, which gave me a better sense of how I needed to deal with them at school. I felt compelled to become the father figure that was missing from their lives as best I could.

Neighborhoods

Although I am in full agreement with the philosophy of "no excuses," I still strongly contend that educators must develop a strong familiarity with the neighborhoods in which their black male students reside. Many black male students gain their sense of identity and belongingness from their neighborhoods—their stature, values, and sense of purpose, as well as their attitudes toward school. For many of them, their neighborhood or even their block is comparable to a badge of honor, and it is incumbent upon you to investigate why.

A few years back, I conducted a professional development workshop at a middle school in the southeastern United States. When I arrived at the school, the principal informed me that before I conducted my session, the administrators and staff were going to board a chartered bus and go on a tour of their students' neighborhoods. I knew that this tour had the potential of helping the teachers to gain valuable insights about their students that they would never gain in the classroom alone. The principal asked me if I'd like to attend, and I didn't hesitate to say yes.

As we boarded the bus, we were greeted by an administrator who served as our tour guide. His role was to explain everything we saw. He showed us the low-income and economically depressed parts of town as well as the middle-income ones; he showed us where the high crime areas were, where drugs were sold, and where various gangs congregated. He also pointed out the distances that students had to travel to and from school.

As we rode back to the school, the teachers discussed the tour. Several of them had grown up in this city themselves, so they expressed no real surprise at anything they saw. Others did express some degree of surprise and concern. I listened attentively as we made our way back to the school. Upon our return, it was time for me to present my workshop. One of the first questions that I asked was, "How many of you learned something new today?" Some of the hands went up. I expressed to the teachers that if they had learned something new from the tour, it might explain some of the deficiencies that they were seeing and experiencing in their classrooms. I told them that in order to know the *whole* student, they must take the initiative on their own to familiarize themselves with their students' neighborhoods.

History and Culture

Malcolm X once stated, "History is best qualified to reward our research" (Shabazz, 1970). As the teacher of black males, have you used their history to make them feel good about themselves and to make them aware of their roles and responsibilities toward themselves, their families, and their communities? What do you know about the history of your black male students? Is it okay in your mind that their culture may be different from your own? Are there any differences between them and the other students in the classroom? If so, how do you deal with these differences? I have learned that many educators at all levels, including those who are themselves black, lack knowledge of black history. Just as one cannot teach what one does not know, one cannot effectively teach *whom* one does not know. When you know your students' history, you know your students.

Your students' history is their collective past, of which they are both product and reflection. History and culture are interrelated: When you study a people's history, you are studying a culture, a way of life. And by familiarizing yourself with the history and culture of your students, you are in a much better position to teach your students their story as well. The best way to learn history is to read about it. To that end, I would like to recommend the following books to get you started:

- *The Miseducation of the Negro,* by Carter G. Woodson
- *Introduction to African Civilizations,* by John G. Jackson
- *The African Origins of Civilization,* by Cheik Anta Diop
- *Nile Valley Contributions to Civilization,* by Anthony T. Browder
- *Destruction of Black Civilization,* by Chancellor Williams
- *Before the Mayflower,* by Lerone Bennett Jr.
- *From Slavery to Freedom,* by John Hope Franklin
- *Introduction to Black Studies,* by Maulana Karenga
- *African American History: A Journey to Liberation,* by Molefi K. Asante
- *They Came Before Columbus,* by Ivan Van Sertima
- *Blacks in Science,* by Ivan Van Sertima
- *Black Inventors of America,* by McKinley Burt Jr.
- *World's Great Men of Color* (Vols. 1 and 2), by J. A. Rogers
- *The Autobiography of Malcolm X,* by Alex Haley
- *King: A Biography,* by David Lewis

Of course, this list is not exhaustive, but it will get you started on your journey of learning the history and culture of your black students and therefore meeting their classroom needs.

CHAPTER 2

Learning About Yourself to Meet Your Black Male Students' Needs

When speaking at conferences and schools, white female educators often ask whether or not I feel that they are at a disadvantage due to their gender and ethnicity. I always answer by relating the following personal experience.

A few years back, I hired a novice teacher who had recently graduated from college to teach at a middle school that was about 98 percent black and about 2 percent Latino and Asian. Less than one week after I had assumed the leadership of this school as its new principal, it was placed on the NCLB-mandated "Persistently Dangerous Schools" list as the most dangerous school in northern New Jersey. This is the environment this novice teacher was stepping into.

The teacher, who was set to teach 7th grade Language Arts, showed up a few weeks before the start of the school year to prepare her classroom. When I visited her room, I was thoroughly impressed: the surroundings were print-rich and engaging, posters on the walls reflected the lives of the students, and the desks were arranged in clusters. I was excited about the prospects for the students assigned to the teacher.

Once the students arrived in the classroom, it was magic from the start. The teacher was in complete control from the beginning, having established herself as the authority figure of the classroom. The students were receptive to her from the very beginning. From that day forward, they loved to be in her presence and learn. They participated in all classroom activities, consistently completed homework assignments, and did well on tests. Achievement levels were outstanding. I was extremely pleased to have the teacher on board as a part of our team.

By the middle of the school year, this novice teacher performed as though she had years of experience behind her. What really stood out for me was her ability to engage her students in student-centered learning and differentiated instruction, while at the same time successfully keeping them on task. She managed to be friendly, firm, and fair all at once. And she was a young, small-framed white woman.

My point is that ethnicity, gender, stature, and even prior experience do not matter; what matters is the teacher's attitude toward her students. A successful teacher believes that her students can and will achieve excellence in her classroom. Such an attitude is a key component for student achievement. Ask yourself the following ten essential questions:

1. Do I see myself as the number-one determinant of my black male students' success or failure?
2. Am I passionate about my role as a teacher of black male students?
3. Have I defined my purpose for teaching my black male students?
4. Do I treat the teaching of my black male students as my mission?
5. Do I have a vision for what I expect my black male students to achieve?
6. Do I set incremental and long-range goals for my black male students?
7. Do I plan each day thoroughly, with a view toward the success of my black male students?
8. Do I have high expectations and standards for my black male students and believe that my students will reach them?

9. Do I see myself as a role model for my black male students, and therefore always conduct myself as a professional?
10. Do I conduct daily self-reflections and self-assessments of my teaching?

Let's now look at each question individually.

Do I See Myself as the Number-One Determinant of My Black Male Students' Success or Failure?

Imagine that you are the number-one determinant of your students' success or failure. When you see yourself as having this level of influence on your students, your students will learn because you will not allow for excuses or exceptions. In your mind, your students are in the best place because they are with you, and you can think of no better person to educate your students than you.

When I was a classroom teacher, if even one student failed an assessment that I administered, I held myself responsible. I would ask myself: What could I have done differently? Did I differentiate my instruction? Did I make the lesson fun, stimulating, and engaging? Did I connect with this particular student during the lesson? Did I check for this student's understanding prior to his taking the test? Did I place a particular emphasis and focus on him to ensure that he was in fact ready to take this assessment and excel? You, too, should ask such questions regularly. Even when all of the students perform well on a given assessment, you should not become complacent. You must continue to challenge yourself to improve in all aspects of your practice.

Am I Passionate About My Role as a Teacher of Black Male Students?

If you are going to experience optimal success, you *must* be passionate about your role as a teacher. You must love arriving at school every morning to greet your students and engage them in sustained rigorous instruction. A sense of passion reverberates across and throughout the classroom, and it becomes contagious to all who are around—especially your students.

I can recall educators who lacked passion for their practice and for their students. It was apparent that they did not enjoy what they did, and it was equally apparent that they did not particularly like children. This attitude manifested itself in low academic performance and undesirable behavior among these teachers' students. You must ensure that your students can actually sense the passion that you have for them by consistently demonstrating your concern for them through your speech and your actions. You must also maintain a high degree of energy and enthusiasm in the classroom; your students must be able to perceive that you are literally excited about their academic growth.

When I was a classroom teacher, I saw my students as my family, with me being the father figure of the classroom. I wanted for them what I would want for my own children. I did whatever it took for them to achieve. My intent was to make men out of my boys. I was passionate about my role and refused to let anything stop me from being successful. In addition to being passionate about their academic achievement, I also knew that I had to be passionate about *them*. If they sensed that my passion for them was sincere, I was in a much better position to connect with them and subsequently help them to raise their achievement levels.

Have I Defined My Purpose for Teaching My Black Male Students?

When I first became an educator, I approached my new journey with a definite sense of purpose. I knew that if I wanted the education of my disadvantaged students to launch them out of poverty, my teaching had to be purposeful. Everything that I did and everything that I said had to be driven by my purpose, which was threefold: to teach my students about their history, to teach them about community and economic development, and to help them to distinguish between being a *male* and being a *man*.

My students' knowledge of their history was quite limited, as it is for most black students. By exposing them to their history, I knew that they would gain a deeper understanding of their roles in life. In terms of community and economic development, I wanted my students to understand that the urban blight that they saw every day did not have to be their permanent reality. I wanted them to understand that they could change their conditions if they were serious about their education and learned all that they could learn. As I taught my students their history, I was able to help them to build a bridge between their collective history and their current realities.

The third aspect of my purpose for teaching was to model manhood for my students. I was keenly aware that the majority of my students did not have a father figure in their homes and that this would potentially have an adverse effect on their social and emotional development. I wanted to be in a position to fill that void in their lives. I wanted to show them how a man—as opposed to a mere male—should conduct himself. (This modeling was just as important for my girls as for my boys; they too had a need to know the difference between a male and a man so that they could distinguish the two in the future.)

Focused on my threefold purpose for teaching didn't mean that everything else that I did in the classroom wasn't important. It simply meant that my purpose for teaching was at the core of my practice, driving my words and actions in the classroom. Have you already taken the time to define your purpose for teaching? If so, what is it? Why do you do what you do every day? What drives your words and actions in your classroom? Do your students know and understand your purpose? Can they relate to it? Do they respond to it?

Do I Treat the Teaching of My Black Male Students as My Mission?

If we want to motivate our black male students to succeed, we as educators must be of the right mindset first. We must genuinely desire their success, and we must go to school mentally prepared to make a tremendous difference in our students' lives every day. In other words, we must be on a mission to ensure that our black male students achieve excellence.

When I speak to the parents of my students at our Back-to-School Open House, I remind them that I am on a mission to ensure that their children achieve excellence and a high-quality, world-class education. Although I am serious about the education of all of the students in my school, I am particularly mindful of the classroom needs of my black male students.

As the classroom teacher of black males, are you on a mission? Is there anything stopping you from achieving your goal of academic excellence for your black males? Do you have a "no excuses" attitude when you are in the classroom with your students? You must make it your business that failure and mediocrity are not options in your classroom.

Do I Have a Vision for What I Expect My Black Male Students to Achieve?

What is your vision for your black male students? On that first day of school of the new school year, as you look into the eyes of each and every one of your black males, you must be able to envision their academic success regardless of the challenges they face; you must be able to envision them performing exceptionally in your classroom, completing all of their homework assignments, and scoring high on your tests and standardized assessments. The more clearly you envision your students' academic success, the likelier it is that it will come true.

Where do you see your students 5, 10, 15 years from now? What is your vision for their growth and development as a result of your instruction? How does your vision for your students translate into their striving to meet your academic expectations? Where do your black males see themselves going as a result of your teaching? Do they envision themselves achieving excellence? Do they feel more confident about themselves and their ability to succeed as a result of your vision for them?

Do I Set Incremental and Long-Range Goals for My Black Male Students?

What are your goals for your black students? Is goal setting part of your overall teaching repertoire? How do you normally measure whether or not your students have met your expectations? Do you write down and post your goals?

Let's suppose that, at the end of the first marking period, you have discovered that a sizable percentage of your black male students are not performing at acceptable proficiency levels. You have decided that you will consequently set incremental goals for all of your students. At this juncture, you might determine a number of students who will meet a certain criterion that you set (e.g., performing well on your next assessment, or making the honor roll by the end of the next marking period). However you set up your goal criteria, what's key is that you have determined goals that you will now be striving for your students to achieve.

Do I Plan Each Day Thoroughly, with a View toward the Success of My Black Male Students?

What is your plan for ensuring that your black male students succeed in your classroom? Have you written down your plan? How often do you refer to your plan? I always say that setting your goals is easy; the challenge is to write a plan of action and adhere to it. Your plan tells you everything you must do to actualize your goals. It is your blueprint, your roadmap. The optimal course of action is to develop an individualized plan for each of your students, predicated on the goals that you set for them. If you do this, the probability for student success increases.

When I think of a plan of action, sports always comes to mind. In sports, a wealth of planning always occurs in preparation for the game, and continues as the game is being played. For example, in football, planning occurs before the game, after every play, on the sidelines, at halftime, after the game, and throughout the week. Much more time is spent planning and preparing than actual playing.

In my professional development workshops with teachers, I frequently make reference to lesson plans and "student plans." Lesson plans are obviously the plans composed of the lessons you will teach during a given week. Your administrator typically expects you to submit a copy of your lesson plans on a weekly basis. Student plans, however, are not typically required by administrators at all. These plans are written by teachers who go the extra mile—those who teach students first, subject areas second. They are developed for individual students, and particularly for those who are at the greatest risk of failure. Teachers who develop student plans clearly understand that if struggling students are going to be able to compete with the higher-achieving students, a considerable amount of time must be spent planning for their success. These plans will be composed of those strategies, efforts, and actions that the teacher must take in order to ensure that their students do well, taking into account the unique challenges (including behavioral issues) facing each individual student. Student-centered teaching, including differentiated instruction, must clearly be the predominant instructional model in your classroom.

Do I Have High Expectations and Standards for My Black Male Students and Believe That My Students Will Reach Them?

Do you believe that your students can and will achieve excellence? Are they aware of your expectations? Each and every day, as your students walk into your classroom, you must expect that they will in fact achieve academic excellence, and that anything less than excellence is unacceptable. Your students need to know that it is simply not an option to give less than their maximum effort.

Of course, your black male students are no different than anyone else, and you should never view them as less capable. They may have unique needs, but they too must be expected to meet the same expectations as everyone else. We all know about the conditions in some of the more troubled inner-city schools across the country. We hear about the violence, the suspension rates, the dropout rates, and the low academic performance. We hear about the "school-to-prison pipeline" in which so many black males find themselves. What is happening between the first and fifth grades that we lose so many of these brilliant boys? I would argue that expectations for them are not as high as they are for others, so students don't have a high standard to which they are compelled to strive.

Recently, I ran into someone on the street who is a friend of one of my former black male students. He told me that this student had a high opinion of me precisely because I was very demanding, and that he had gone on to a successful life.

As important as it is to have high expectations, it is probably more important that you actually believe that your black males will reach and exceed your expectations. Students can tell when their teachers believe in them.

Do I See Myself as a Role Model for My Black Male Students, and Therefore Always Conduct Myself as a Professional?

Do you consider yourself to be a role model for your students? Do your students consider you to be a positive role model for them? Do you welcome your role model status? Whether you are a man or a woman, you are a role model for your students. Your students are listening to every word that you utter and watching every move that you make. It is one thing to tell students what you expect of them; it is an entirely different thing for them to see expected behaviors being modeled by the people whom they respect.

It saddens me when I hear students proclaim that they would never want to become teachers because they see teaching as insignificant or lacking prestige. If we are going to attract students into the teaching profession, we must demonstrate to them that what we do is indeed significant. We can begin by dressing like professionals. If you tell your students that it is important to dress professionally for job interviews and in professional settings, you must also demonstrate the same in your classroom environment. Doing so sends a message to the students that what we do every day is important, which in turn implies to the students that their education is important as well.

Do I Conduct Daily Self-Reflections and Self-Assessments of My Teaching?

Do you take the time to reflect upon and assess your school day? At what point of the day do you conduct your self-reflection and self-assessment? How do you determine what worked and what needs to be adjusted? Once you make your determination, what is the next step? At the end of the school day, after all of the students have left for the afternoon, there are a lot of activities that teachers engage in to prepare for the next day. These activities might include grading and filing student work, revising lesson plans, posting student work samples on the bulletin board, and calling parents. I would like to suggest another activity: self-reflection and self-assessment.

To continue growing professionally and to become better at what you do, you must devote a portion of your afternoons to silent time during which you sit at your desk and do nothing but reflect upon everything that happened from the time you arrived that day to the time that your students left. You should simply "run the videotape" of the day in your mind, without being judgmental. Once you have completed your reflection, you should consider what worked and what didn't work. Think about why the things that worked worked, and why those that didn't work didn't. Assess yourself honestly, and think about what you could have done better.

Once you have completed your self-reflection and self-assessment, you should record your findings in a journal to which you can refer back later. You should also set goals for the next day based upon your self-assessment. This routine will help focus your attention on successfully meeting the classroom needs of your students.

CHAPTER 3

Three Crises

There is a wealth of background information that you must know to effectively meet the classroom needs of black males. You cannot just go into a classroom and start teaching. There are too many variables at play that have the potential of inhibiting both teaching and learning, some of which I would go so far as to call crises. You are not necessarily in a position to correct all of the crises that your students encounter; some are in fact well beyond your control. The purpose of this chapter is to discuss three major crises that all teachers need to be aware of, as they have direct implications on the potential for optimal learning in your classroom.

The Community Crisis

Most of us are familiar with the proverb "It takes a village to raise a child." I am a firm believer in this proverb. It is ideal when large numbers of people work collaboratively on behalf of children—when, no matter which way the children turn, there is an adult present to keep them in check and to hold them accountable.

I can recall knowing literally every adult on my entire block when I was growing up in New Jersey during the 1960s and 1970s. The adults on my block knew all of the children on my block as well. No matter where we went or which way we turned, there was always some adult whom we knew nearby. None of us were allowed to leave the block. We didn't want to; everything that we needed was there. When it was time to come inside, our parents did not have to concern themselves with where we were. All they had to do was go to the front porch and either call out our names or ring a bell and we'd come running.

I do not recall one of us ever being disrespectful toward an adult. The adults on my block certainly would not have tolerated it. Our parents knew that we were in good hands when we walked out of the front door. They knew that the other adults on the block were going to hold us to the same standard of conduct that our own parents did. We also knew that if we were caught acting inappropriately, they would report our behavior to our parents immediately. This was nonnegotiable.

The "village" concept was fully operational during those years. Adults understood their roles, and everyone worked collaboratively toward the growth and development of the neighborhood children. Although I lived in an urban setting, I have no recollection of the gangs, drugs, or violence with which my students today have to contend on a regular basis.

Times have changed dramatically since I was a youngster. Many children nowadays don't know any of their neighbors, and can engage in destructive behaviors without anyone reporting it to their parents. Gangs have taken over many urban streets, selling drugs and guns out in the open. Too many black boys end up joining these gangs so that they can remain safe in their own neighborhoods. The community as a whole subsequently becomes unsafe, with residents having to look over their shoulders constantly. Everyone pretty much knows who's doing what, but the code on the streets strictly prohibits "snitching." Because little gets reported, parents are therefore oblivious to what their children are doing in the neighborhood.

Urban communities across the country are in a state of crisis, and hundreds of thousands of black males across the country are products of these communities. Teachers are obviously not in positions to correct this crisis, but they must be acutely aware of their students' realities.

Before I give presentations to students at school assemblies, I ask the administrators whether they have a gang problem in their school. They invariably respond that they do not, although there are isolated gang members in the school. I then ask them how many students they suspect might belong to gangs. They typically reply that it is a small percentage. Then, during my presentation, I ask the students: "How many of you are affiliated with a gang?" Typically, about 90 percent of the hands go up.

Clearly, the layers of damage that must be permeated to rectify this crisis are many. In some cases, they are so overwhelming that many teachers leave the profession prematurely because they feel that they simply cannot connect with their black male students. You must therefore be prepared to contend with the repercussions of the community crisis in your classroom, such as a lack of motivation to succeed, undesirable behaviors, and poor academic performance.

Of course, the inner cities of the United States continue to produce an abundance of extraordinary people who are doing extraordinary things in their communities and with their lives. Many black males strive to achieve academic excellence in school despite experiencing the same challenges as their less successful peers. The difference is that they are clear about the *purpose* of education; they are on a *mission* to make their education work for them, and they have a *vision* for where they expect their education to take them. They are committed to what they want out of life. Many of these young men go on to some of the best colleges in the country and turn out to be major success stories. Because we tend to focus on the problems of the inner city, success stories tend to be overlooked—even by the black males who would most benefit from exposure to them.

The Family Crisis

Ideally, black males should be going home to fathers or father figures as well as mothers. Although mothers can potentially do a superb job of teaching their sons about being a man, only a man can truly model manhood. When males are absent from the lives of black school-aged males, mothers, schools, or the streets become the substitute fathers. I believe that classroom teachers must be aware of this problem in order to know the realities that their students face.

The Self-Crisis

The third and most crucial crisis is the "self-crisis." Due to the effects of the community and family crises, many black male students enter school with unresolved issues concerning their communities and families. I contend that as long as we continue to focus on content areas first and students second, we will continue to get the same results we are trying so hard to improve.

Simply put, the self-crisis is the breakdown of the individual. It manifests itself in the following categories:

- Self-image
- Self-esteem
- Self-discipline
- Self-respect
- Self-actualization

In classrooms across the country, far too many teachers are forced to address these manifestations of the self-crisis at the expense of their students' content area learning activities.

Self-Image

How do your students see themselves? If they are to succeed in school, they must see themselves as possessing all of the necessary tools to achieve whatever they set their minds on achieving. To that end, they must develop positive and productive self-images. To gauge the self-images of the black males in your classroom, you must ask them how they see themselves and monitor their behaviors closely.

Imagine trying to teach an individual who doesn't see himself capable of achieving success. For example, suppose you have a young man in your classroom whose self-image is that of a "thug." If this is how he sees himself, it is going to be very difficult to successfully teach him math and science. He has defined himself in a way that runs counter to everything you are attempting to instill in your students. His focus is not on learning, but rather on living up to his definition of himself. Your role, consequently, is to guide him toward changing his self-image so that he can become a productive student in your classroom.

A few years ago, while engaged in an intense conversation with several black male teenagers, one of them said to me, "We are just [n-words]. We do what [n-words] do. We're just [n-words] from the 'hood." Now, this attitude obviously illustrates a very destructive self-image. You must attempt to eradicate this type of negativity regularly at every opportunity. As long as your black males see themselves and each other as n-words, they will never experience optimal success in their classrooms. I might add that far too many young males have embraced this horrible word as a "term of endearment." They argue that it does not carry the same meaning that it once did, and even spell it differently, replacing the "-er" with "-a," "-as," or "-az." My position is that this word is absolutely unacceptable, regardless of its spelling. As the classroom teacher, you must relentlessly drive this message home.

Ultimately, while students are in your classroom, they must actually see themselves as being positive and productive. They must get to a point where they feel empowered to excel. Your objective must therefore be to empower your black male students; you must give them the power and authority to excel. You must consistently encourage them to see themselves as being serious about learning, focused on achieving excellence, diligent in their efforts, disciplined in their actions, and resilient after their setbacks.

Self-Esteem

How do your students feel about themselves? I often tell teachers their role as a motivator is at the core of their practice; teachers cannot effectively educate their students if they have not first determined how to keep them motivated and inspired about learning. As you strive toward successfully motivating and educating your students, your ultimate goal is to empower them to believe that they now possess the ability to achieve anything in life that they set their minds on achieving. To reach this goal, you must focus on inspiring your students to feel good about themselves.

Although a young man with a positive and productive self-image will resultantly feel very good about himself, the same can be true of someone with a negative or destructive self-image, particularly if he has been embraced by peers who support negativity and destruction. The latter situation is incredibly difficult for you to rectify due to the overwhelming influence of peer pressure. You must therefore remain mindful of the reality that a student with high self-esteem does not necessarily have a positive self-image. Your objective must be for your young men to have both a positive self-image and high self-esteem.

To increase the probability that your black males feel good about themselves, you must strive to consistently remind them how special they are, how intelligent they are, and how capable they are of achieving excellence in your classroom. You must remind them regularly that you believe in them and that you are confident that they can achieve whatever they set their minds on achieving. Sustained positive communication and encouragement must be the norm in your classroom.

Self-Discipline

Are your students in control of themselves? You must consistently encourage your students to always do what is right, required, and expected. They must be able to demonstrate to themselves and others that yes, they are actually in control of themselves. Your students must be responsible and able to hold themselves accountable. They must develop the discipline to

- Meet all school and classroom expectations.
- Complete all of their homework assignments and study for success.
- Read daily beyond the books that are assigned to them.
- Listen carefully to prepare themselves for success.
- Manage their time effectively.
- Engage in daily self-reflection and self-assessment.
- Make good, sound, wise decisions.
- Consistently be both patient and persistent.

- Accept responsibility for their own failure and mediocrity.
- Engage in appropriate school and classroom behaviors.
- Resolve conflicts peacefully.

Self-Respect

Do your students bring honor to themselves? I learned very early in my career that many of the problems associated with keeping my black males focused on education were rooted in their lack of self-respect.

One common example of a lack of self-respect among black males is the tendency to wear sagging pants. Why is it that black males all over the country are so intent upon wearing their pants and shorts far below their waistline? Why do they not feel any shame in displaying their underwear to those around them? I see this as a blatant lack of self-respect. As the classroom teacher, it is incumbent upon you to address this behavior every time you observe it. Your students must be made to understand that "sagging" in your classroom and the school is absolutely unacceptable. The problem is so enormous now that it has even crossed over into other ethnic groups, and it has crossed gender lines in some cases as well.

In addition to helping students to respect themselves, it is important to also help them to:

- Demonstrate respect toward their male peers.
- Demonstrate respect toward their female peers.
- Demonstrate respect toward their teachers.
- Make a positive difference in their school.
- Accept obstacles as challenges to be overcome.

- Surround themselves with other positive people.
- Always engage in acceptable and appropriate school behaviors.
- Avoid the use of negative and destructive language and speech.

Self-Actualization

How are your students maximizing their potential? It is my belief that young black men are born highly capable of achieving excellence, but somehow lose their way in the early grades. To ensure that black males continue to excel through 12th grade and beyond, we must keep them inspired. As their teacher, it is your responsibility to make them aware of their inherent ability while also helping them to bring it out. You must therefore consistently push and challenge them to maximize their potential. Mediocrity cannot be an option. You must hold your students accountable for achieving nothing less than excellence.

In the following chapter, I will examine the self-crisis in depth and offer potential solutions for teachers.

CHAPTER 4

"Who Am I?"

It was a Monday morning, the start of a new school week. In my role as principal of an urban high school, I had just finished my morning announcements, which are a tremendously important part of my morning routine as they set the tone for the start of the school day. I was now ready to make my rounds.

My first stop was a senior-level U.S. History class. I saw the students entering the classroom as the teacher greeted them at the door. I followed the students in. When they got into the room, they opened their notebooks and began to work on their "do now." My plan was to stay in the room for no more than two minutes, as I wanted to visit every room in the building before the first block ended. Once the students completed their work, the teacher went over their answers. The class then proceeded with the lesson of the day, which was to be a continuation of the previous week's lesson on slavery in the United States. The focus today was on the methods of buying and selling African slaves during the colonial period. Part of the movie *Roots* was to be shown so that the students could better visualize the lesson. I found myself curious as to how the students might react to the movie, so I decided that I'd stay for a while.

The teacher started the movie. All students were focused on the screen. In this particular scene, which concerned slaves being sold at auction, the lead character, Kunta Kinte, was being looked over by a potential buyer. As the students watched the scene, I payed close attention to the black males in the classroom. I wanted to see their reactions, if any. At the end of the scene, the teacher engaged the students in a discussion on what they had just seen.

The males were clearly the most vocal in a class composed of black and Latino males and females. They said things such as, "They wouldn't have done that to me; I would have fought back." As the discussion unfolded, it became quite evident to me that many of the students did not perceive the continuum between what they had seen and their current realities. They did not see themselves as being part of a continuum that started with their ancestors in Africa. They knew that they were black and therefore descendants of slaves, but their understanding was superficial at best. They did not see or make the connection in a substantive way, which made me think of the self-crisis that so many of them are grappling with. I didn't sense the seriousness or even anger in the discussion that I would have expected at this grade level.

As I sat in the classroom observing the fascinating discussion led by an outstanding educator, I couldn't help but think back to my own school experiences, when I myself grappled with a self-crisis. During my high school years, I had gotten to the point that I could no longer see education as the key to my success. I couldn't see how learning the various subjects that I was taking in school would translate into my becoming a successful adult. These sentiments consequently had an adverse effect in my grades.

I too had seen *Roots* as a youngster. I saw it when it was first aired in the 1970s. My mother required me to watch it in its entirety. I, like my students, did not make the connection at that time between the story portrayed in the movie and my own circumstances. I only made that connection years later.

By the time I graduated from high school, I was so lost that I didn't know which way to turn. Although I wound up going to a four-year college, I was still clueless as to my life's purpose. I lacked motivation and an earnest desire to succeed; indeed, I did not know if I really had what it took to succeed. I was not yet at the point where I understood that I had the power to determine my own success and destiny.

This is where so many of our black males are today. They are highly capable and have the potential for greatness. As I tell them all of the time, the world is theirs; all they have to do is reach out and grab it. But they must first be made aware of who and what they are. They must connect with their historical past. They must be inspired to strive to achieve excellence. They must possess the necessary motivation to succeed.

During my first week of college, I decided to venture into the library just to familiarize myself with it. I knew that if I was going to be academically successful, I must at least acclimate myself with the library. As I journeyed aimlessly throughout the stacks, I wound up in the Black Studies section. One book protruded from the shelf, catching my attention. I grabbed it, sat down, and began to read it. It was entitled *To Kill a Black Man* by Louis Lomax. I found the title intriguing because it reflected the reality of violence in the black community.

The book was about the lives of Dr. Martin Luther King Jr. and Malcolm X. What I knew about both of these men collectively at that time could fit on the head of a pin, which speaks volumes about my education up to that point. I was so excited about what I was reading that I read the book in about a day or two. As I read it, I felt myself transforming with the turn of each page. I literally felt myself coming into my manhood as I learned about these two great men. As a result, I now recommend this book to anyone with even a single black male in his or her classroom.

Reading the book, I was particularly intrigued by the life of Malcolm X. I subsequently got myself a copy of Alex Haley's *Autobiography of Malcolm X* and read it as quickly as I could. I found myself profoundly fascinated by his complete evolution from a very young boy all the way to his final day. I can remember thinking that this book should be required reading for all black males. Malcolm personified what a man can do when he has purpose for his life. Once I finished reading that book, I felt that I knew what I wanted to become. I now felt that I knew who I was, what I was, and why I was, even though there remained a tremendous amount of reading for me to do. I also developed a sense of purpose for my educational pursuit, and a vision of where I expected my education to take me. I fervently wanted to become an urban elementary school teacher.

As the story goes, when Malcolm was a street hustler, he was ultimately apprehended, arrested, and sent to prison. During his six-year incarceration, he read everything that he could get his hands on from the prison library, with an emphasis on black history. Malcolm literally educated himself while he was in prison, by reading books voraciously. I was inspired by Malcolm's example. I too developed an appetite for reading. I wanted to read everything that Malcolm read while he was in prison. Over the next 10 years, I read everything that I could get my hands on relative to black history: *Black Man of the Nile,* by Yosef ben-Jochannan; *Introduction to African Civilization,* by John G. Jackson; *African Origins of Civilization,* by Cheik Anta Diop; *Stolen Legacy,* by George G. M. James; *Destruction of Black Civilization,* by Chancellor Williams; *World's Great Men of Color,* by J. A. Rogers; and *Blacks in Science* by Ivan Van Sertima, just to name a few. While maintaining a solid A average in all of my coursework, I was able to read pretty much a book per week. I was on a mission to learn everything that I felt I should have learned back in grade school. I rapidly got to the point where I could answer the question, "Who am I?" I did not consider my coursework to be as difficult as I used to, because I had now made a connection with my past; I now understood that I was a descendent of greatness and firmly believed that I could achieve anything that I set my mind on achieving. I had never before felt so good about who I was as a black male, and I had never before felt the confidence in myself that I was now feeling. My study of black history provided me with the foundation that I so desperately needed in my academic development.

My transformation actually occurred on five distinct levels:

First, I began to believe in myself. As a result of learning all that I did over a relatively short period, I made a personal connection with a history that I did not know existed.

Second, I developed a sense of purpose. No longer was I wandering aimlessly. My life now had meaning. I knew what I wanted to do with my life: I wanted to teach. I wanted to enlighten young people by exposing them to the same information that awakened me. I felt that if I could provide them with some of what I learned, I could change their outlooks on life as well.

Third, I came to understand my obligation to excel. Prior to my reading, I was unaware of the struggles that had been waged to bring about equality for black Americans. I now understood that I too had an obligation to be the best student that I could be.

Fourth, I developed a determination to succeed. Nothing could now stop me from achieving my dreams. I knew that my future students were going to be in good hands because I was determined to become a great educator.

Finally, I developed a sense of vision. I saw myself becoming a great educator before even embarking upon the journey. I was able to envision the students assigned to me striving to achieve excellence. I even envisioned myself one day becoming the teacher of the year, which did in fact happen a few years later.

I graduated from Kean College *summa cum laude.* I was so inspired by my reading of black history that it translated into my striving to achieve academic excellence. The books I was reading enabled me to make a connection with my history that I had never even conceived of before. I now knew of the greatness of my ancestors. This rich history made me feel that I could achieve anything that I set my mind on achieving, which explained the rapid turnaround of my grades. I made a solid connection between my present reality and my historical past. I had learned through books that black people had accomplished great things throughout the course of history. I felt an obligation to continue the legacy that was left for my generation.

Not long after receiving my undergraduate degree, I took graduate level courses in education and started my teaching career as a 5th grade elementary school teacher in Brooklyn, New York. I had now emerged out of my self-crisis. I knew who and what I was in history. I felt good about who and what I was. I had developed an attitude that would later enable me to soar as an educator.

For over 20 years, I have maintained that black children in general, and black males in particular, will find themselves at the lower end of the achievement gap as long as we continue to label their academic deficiencies as reading and math problems. These deficiencies are merely symptoms of the self-crisis discussed in Chapter 3, which too often goes unaddressed in our schools.

Many educators confuse the manifestations of self-crisis with the cause. For example, educators typically speak of black males exhibiting low self-esteem or destructive self-images. They contend that if the students had higher self-esteem or productive self-images, they would perform much better in class. Consequently, further investments are made toward addressing the manifestations of the crisis. But the manifestations are not the problem; they, too, are symptoms.

If we are ever to solve the crisis of the black male, schools and districts across the country must earnestly begin to address the root cause of the self-crisis: self-identity.

Self-Identity

In my professional development workshops, I engage my audiences in an exercise in which I provide a participant with a mirror and ask him to look at his reflection. I then tell him to imagine that he does not recognize the person in the reflection, and to hold that thought for a few seconds. Then I tell him to imagine not being able to recognize anyone or anything in his life. I ask him to concentrate hard on this notion for a few seconds, and then I ask him how it feels. I then tell the group that historically and culturally, this exercise is representative of what black children are experiencing in their lives every day. Due to the omission, distortion, or marginalization of their history, they arrive to school everyday with historical and cultural amnesia. They do not know who they are historically and culturally in a definitive way, which adversely affects their academic performance.

Why would academic coursework be important to a student who is struggling with issues of historical and cultural amnesia, and therefore self-identity? How can you really feel good about yourself if you don't know who you are in a historical context? If you lack a historical context of who you are on the world stage, how can you see yourself as a winner?

Many have argued that the absence of black history in curriculums is a major cause of poor academic performance among black males. Perkins (2005), for example, talks about how the suppression of black history has left black youths in the United States completely ignorant of their past and consequently prone to identifying with almost any trend that has popular appeal. The absence of black history results in the inability to definitively answer the question, "Who am I?"

Each of us has both a self-identity and several different collective identities. A person's self-identity answers the question, "Who am I?"—that is, it distinguishes him from everyone else in the world and comprises all of the qualities that make him who he is. By contrast, a person's collective identity comprises the qualities that make up the various groups to which he belongs, such as his gender group, ethnic group, work group, social groups, and so on.

In my presentations, one of the first questions that I ask young black men is, "Who are you?" Invariably, most of them do not know. Because they have not been exposed to black history, they are not in touch with their collective selves. Although they are aware that they are black and typically gravitate to others who look like them, the fact remains that far too many of them lack knowledge of who they really are. We must get young black males to the point where they can definitively answer the following five questions that speak to their self-identity:

- Who am I?
- What am I?
- Why am I?
- What is my purpose?
- What is my vision?

How do you think your black males would answer these questions if you asked them today? To what extent would their answers be attributable to your current instructional practices? What strategies would you employ in your future instruction to further help them with these questions?

Black males must live African-centered lives if they are to view the world from the perspective of who they are historically. As the classroom teacher, you must help them to develop a self-identity as black males by exposing them to their collective history. You must teach them who they are, both historically and culturally, across all content areas. Their knowledge of who they are will become the foundation upon which they stand, and will help them to gain a better awareness of why they attend school in the first place.

Too many educators are spending inordinate amounts of time addressing issues associated with self-esteem, self-image, self-discipline, self-respect, and self-actualization without first addressing the issue of self-identity. When students enter school with a distorted self-identity, teachers are forced to spend time addressing the consequences thereof, such as negative or destructive self-image, low self-esteem, poor self-discipline, lack of self-respect, and an unwillingness to maximize one's potential through self-actualization.

An African proverb states, "I am, because we are; and because we are, I am." In the African tradition, there is more of an emphasis on the collective than the individual. In an African-centered context, then, the questions listed above can just as easily be restated to reflect the entire black community:

- Who are we?
- What are we?
- Why are we?
- What is our purpose?
- What is our vision?

Who Am I? (Who Are We?)

After starting my reading journey of black history in 1984, I became increasingly agitated with the completion of each book. This was not because I didn't enjoy what I was reading; I was actually fascinated by everything that I was learning. I became angry because I couldn't understand why I hadn't been exposed to this information in the classroom when I was in grade school. I quickly came to the realization that this lack of early exposure to black history was a major reason why so many young black males had such a lack of interest in school. We simply didn't see reflections of ourselves in our teachers' instruction, so learning lacked relevance for many of us.

If your students cannot connect what they're taught to their unique experiences as black males, their motivation and desire to learn diminishes greatly. In all of the subject areas that you teach, you must ensure that your black males can see themselves at the heart of your instruction.

As a classroom teacher of black males, you must prepare yourself to help them answer the same question: "Who am I?" They must come to the point where they genuinely believe in themselves, have developed a sense of purpose for their lives, understand their obligations to excel, possess the will to succeed, and have a vision of themselves achieving academic excellence.

Your black males are not the only ones who should learn about their history; most of your students are probably just as ill-informed about the black experience, so it is important to expose them to this history as well.

As your students become increasingly aware of their history, they will learn of the many fields in which black males have already excelled—not just sports and entertainment. Still, students who wish to become professional athletes or entertainers should not be discouraged from their dreams, but rather encouraged to create backup plans. In addition, be sure to ask your students who aspire to become professional athletes questions such as these:

- How hard are you working toward achieving your dream?
- How many hours per day do you spend perfecting your craft?
- How hard do you work in practice?

These students need to understand that in order to become a professional athlete they will have to work diligently, as there is enormous competition, but a limited number of available opportunities.

What Am I? (What Are We?)

Whereas the question of *who* we are speaks to our historical-cultural identity, the question of *what* we are speaks to our gender identity.

Black males must have opportunities to learn what it means to be a young man, including the requisite roles and responsibilities.

I speak at all-male programs as often as I can, and one of the topics that I spend a lot of time addressing is the distinction between a man and a male. I teach young black males that in the African tradition, a boy is only considered a man after he has undergone training to become one. He is removed from the village and taught how to become a man by other men; then, once he has passed all of the required tests, he reenters the village as a man, assuming all of the responsibilities that go along with his new role.

To help your black males to cope with and ultimately free themselves of their self-crisis, you must help them to understand not only who they are, but what they are as well.

Why Am I? (Why Are We?)

Whenever I speak at juvenile detention centers, I find it depressing to see so many black males with whom we as educators failed to connect. Now they languish behind bars. The corrections officers usually bring them to the gym and have them seated in chairs that are arranged in lecture format. As I look at the young men, their innocence is easily detectable—and yet they are now in prison jumpsuits. As I look deep into their eyes without giving the impression that I am staring, I can see not only their innocence, but their pain as well. These young men are bright, and they know it. They know that they have no business in this place, but due to circumstances, here they dwell.

Once, as the young men were being led by the corrections officers into the gym, I heard a young man yell out, "Mr. Kafele!" He then shared with a detainee close by that I used to be his middle school principal. His presence was a harsh personal reminder for me of the work that still needs to be done. As I looked at this young man and eventually engaged him in a brief conversation, I began to question myself. I asked myself what I could have done differently to keep this young man out of a juvenile detention center. I wished that I had made a better connection with him while I had him in middle school.

At this same session, after my formal presentation, I had a brief question-and-answer session, during which one of the young men said to me, "Nothing's going to change for us. This is how it is in the 'hood—always has been, always will be." I refused and continue to refuse to accept this explanation as my reality, but too many youths actually believe it to be true. In this young man's mind, he was in the detention center because *that was where he was supposed to be.* In his mind, detention centers are where young black males wind up.

Of course, I understand that we are not going to save every young black male, but we must maintain the attitude that we will. Our expectations for them must always be sky-high. As long as we maintain the right attitude, we increase the probability that our students' success will in fact become reality.

Black males need to know and understand why their present conditions are as they are. By exposing them to their history, we can help them gain such valuable insight. Without this understanding, they will continue to accept incarceration as a natural condition rather than as the consequence of centuries of racism. Having had the opportunity to visit many inner cities across the country, I have seen these consequences firsthand. No matter what city or state I visit, the story is always the same: too many black males are not living up to their potential. Who's going to motivate these young men to strive to maximize their potential in the classroom? Who's going to convince them that there is a world out there beyond the blocks that they live on, and that they have access to it if they make the right decisions along the way? The responsibility rests squarely on the shoulders of educators.

According to Noguera (2008), many students learn about race in school through what he calls the hidden or informal curriculum. He states:

> For African American males, who are more likely than any other group to be subjected to negative forms of treatment in school, the message is clear: individuals of their race and gender may excel in sports, but not math or history. The location of African American males within schools—in remedial classes or waiting for punishment outside of the principal's office—and the roles they perform within school suggest that they are good at playing basketball or rapping, but debating, writing for the school newspaper, or participating in the science club is strictly out of bounds. Such activities are out of bounds not just because African American males may perceive them as being inconsistent with who they think they are, but also because there simply are not enough examples of individuals who manage to participate in such activities without compromising their sense of self. (p. 31)

You must make your black males understand that they have the ability to achieve anything in life that they set their sights on achieving; the choice is theirs, and the power is in their hands. You need to effectively guide them in the right direction. If you fail in your efforts, the probability for their success diminishes with each succeeding year.

It is important to also teach your students how to think critically and analytically. As they begin to grapple with the "why" of their conditions by studying black history, they must learn to look at the world differently and draw conclusions on their own, based on what they have learned about their collective selves. As Carter G. Woodson (1933), considered by many to be the father of black history, stated in one of his most important works, *The Miseducation of the Negro*:

> When you control a man's thinking, you do not have to worry about his actions. You do not have to tell him not to stand here or go yonder. He will find his 'proper place' and will stay in it. You do not need to send him to the back door. He will go without being told. In fact, if there is no back door, he will cut one for his special benefit. His education makes it necessary. (p. xiii)

What Is My Purpose? (What Is Our Purpose?)

In my roles as both a classroom teacher and a building principal, I have often posted a sign on the wall that reads: "When the black history books are written 100 years from now, what will be written about you?" This is a question of purpose. It is one of the vehicles that I use to get my students to start thinking about their roles in life.

You must ensure that your students are arriving at your classroom every day with a sense of purpose for being there. This sense of purpose evolves out of their understanding of who they are, what they are, and why they are. As long as they are coming to school with no sense of purpose, they are essentially just showing up and taking up space. Ideally, we want them to come to school because they genuinely want to be there and they are clear about what their education can and will produce for them.

I have observed many black males who are clueless about their purpose. In many cases, no one has taken the time to help them to define what their purpose is, so these students wander about aimlessly with no specific direction, goals, or plans of action. When one lacks purpose, direction, goals, and a plan, one is doing no more than simply existing. Black males must be encouraged to do more than simply exist; they must be encouraged to strive toward achieving academic excellence in their classrooms.

When I was a classroom teacher, I required my students to set goals for each of their subject areas. This goal setting gave them a sense of purpose for each of their subjects. It gave each of them a target to aim for and therefore a purpose for being there. I provided each student with a sheet of paper on which they were to list their goals for each subject area in the form of a grade, and develop a written strategy for achieving each goal. I called these papers "goal sheets." Each goal sheet was posted on the "Wall of Fame" in my classroom and changed each marking period, depending on the actual grade that was achieved.

The key for this process to work is ensuring that students' goals are attainable. For example, if a student gets Ds or Fs in math, an A would not be a realistic goal, but a C would be. Once the student reaches this goal, he might set his next goal as a B. He should think of his goals as stairs and go one or two steps at a time.

The "goal sheet" strategy must be well thought out if it is going to work. It should address what your students will do to achieve their goals both in class and at home. In my case, the strategy served as an accountability measure, as it enabled me to hold my students accountable for each of the goals that they set. If I saw that a student was deviating from his plan of action, I would take him to the Wall of Fame and remind him of the goals that he set and the plan that he said that he was going to adhere to in order to achieve them.

When I became a principal, I decided that I would continue to have my students set goals at the building-level. Each student was responsible for a "goal card"—that is, an index card on which they were to write their goals for each of their subjects, plus in-class and at-home plans for achieving them. The cards would be posted on each classroom wall and changed at the end of each marking period.

According to Davis (2005), goals should be SMART: specific, measurable, achievable, realistic, and time-oriented. The more your students work on achieving their goals, the more clearly they will see the correlation between purpose, goal setting, and high academic performance.

What Is My Vision? (What Is Our Vision?)

Typically, when I conduct lectures and keynotes, I speak extensively about the members of the audience developing a vision for their success. I tell them that I want them to go beyond dreaming and imagining. I want them to be able to actually envision themselves achieving whatever they set their minds on—to see their success in their mind's eye. At elementary and middle school graduations, I have the graduates close their eyes and lead them through a process of envisioning themselves progressing through each level of schooling, all the way to receiving their doctorate degree. At each level, I ask the graduates, "Can you see it? Can you feel it? Does it make you feel good?" After each question, the graduates yell out, "Yes!" After we reach the doctoral level, I tell them that they have reached that point because they dared to see themselves achieving their degrees in their mind's eye.

The same applies in the classroom with your black males: they must be able to envision their success before even embarking upon it. Many of us fail to ever reach our dreams because we lacked the courage to envision them. As the classroom teacher, you must inspire your black males to see themselves making the honor roll on the first day of school. You must convince them of how talented and capable they are. They need you to inspire them to have a vision of where they are headed. The key is being consistent and persistent with your encouragement.

Cultural Relevance in the Classroom

To fully address the self-crisis, curriculum and instruction must be culturally relevant, culturally appropriate, culturally responsive, and culturally sensitive to the learner. We want our students to be able to identify with and relate to what they are learning. Your lessons must be developed with the unique needs of your black male learners in mind. They want to be able to see how the information they are being exposed to relates to them and applies to their world.

Gay (2000) defines *culturally responsive teaching* as "using the cultural knowledge, prior experiences, frames of reference, and performance styles of ethnically diverse students to make learning encounters more relevant to and effective for them. It teaches to and through the strengths of these students. It is culturally validating and affirming" (p. 29). As Howard (2006) notes, "We must know our students well, both for the purpose of building relationships that work, and also for the purpose of designing curriculum and pedagogical strategies that are responsive to, and honoring of, our students' actual lived experiences. There is no work more complex, and there is no work more important, than this" (p. 132).

As the classroom teacher of black males, you must maintain a focus on ensuring that their needs are being met throughout every lesson that you teach. Culturally responsive teaching will require that you use your students' culture as an important source of their overall education (Tatum, 2005). Let's look specifically at the four broad subject areas of social studies, language arts, math, and science.

Cultural Relevance in Social Studies

Are you aware of the black influence in various eras of U.S. history? Are your students aware? If so, is their knowledge attributable to your instruction? If not, do you shoulder any of the blame for their lack of knowledge? Black Americans were prominently influential during the following eras, movements, and events:

- The Revolutionary War
- The Industrial Revolution
- The Abolitionist Movement
- The Civil War
- Reconstruction
- Westward Expansion
- World Wars I and II
- The Civil Rights Movement

In addition to learning about black influence in the United States, your black students also need to learn about their African past. They need to know about life in Africa before the period of enslavement. They need to know of the greatness of their ancestors; for example, they need to know that there were thousands of years of African civilization prior to the slave trade. They need to know that African men played major roles in the spread of civilization throughout the centuries. You must make your students aware of the roles their ancestors played in the development of writing, mathematics, science, engineering, architecture, and astronomy.

Cultural Relevance in Language Arts

Your black male students need to be exposed to reading material that allows them to see themselves from a historical vantage point. They need maximum exposure to black Harlem Renaissance writers, for example, such as Langston Hughes, James Baldwin, Zora Neale Hurston, James Weldon Johnson, Claude McKay, Countee Cullen, Alain Locke, Gwendolyn Bennett, and Anne Spencer. They also should learn about contemporary writers who are writing about the black experience. When students find their reading material relevant to their lives, their reading comprehension is bound to improve.

In addition to having them read, you must also require your students to write about the themes in the books they are reading. They should be encouraged to write critiques, analyses, reactions, and summaries. They should also be encouraged to write original pieces about the black male experience.

Cultural Relevance in Math

Many aspects of math have their origins in Africa. For example, algebra, geometry, trigonometry, and calculus can all be traced back to their African origins (Van Seritima, 1989; Zaslavsky, 1979). Your students need to learn about these origins; by learning that their ancestors played major roles toward the creation, development, and dissemination of mathematics, they become better able to take ownership of their math instruction. You should teach lessons on black male mathematicians, so that your black male students can see that men who look like them can and have excelled in math.

Cultural Relevance in Science

Black men were behind many of the world's great inventions, including the carbon thread filament of the light bulb, the automatic transmission of the automobile, the portable x-ray machine, the refrigerated truck, the third rail of a train track, automatic lubrication of machines, the gas mask, the automatic traffic signal, and the automatic car wash (Burt Jr., 1969). Your black males need to know of these and the hundreds of other inventions by black men. They need to see that it is nothing new for black men to excel in science. Once they internalize this fact, they are much likelier to develop African-centered identities beyond the realms of athletics and entertainment.

CHAPTER 5

Developing a Young Men's Empowerment Program

In Chapter 4, I discussed activities that should take place in the classroom between the teacher and the students. In this chapter, I will discuss activities that should occur outside of the traditional classroom. I refer to these activities as the Young Men's Empowerment Program.

In October of 1995, when I was an elementary school teacher, over one million black men from all over the country came together in Washington, D.C., for the Million Man March. The purpose of this march was for black men to come together in a tremendous showing of unity. As a relatively new teacher, I was excited to be a part of the march. I couldn't wait to get back to my students to share the experience of being in one place with over a million black men in a show of unity with absolutely no conflicts or violence.

When I got back to school the next day, I planned to recreate the march on a small scale with all of the male students that I taught— about 75 total. I got all my black males together and we spent half a day discussing issues related to being a black male. At the conclusion, to formally end our session, we engaged in the following pledge:

> *I pledge always to demonstrate respect for myself.*
> *I pledge always to demonstrate respect for my peers.*
> *I pledge always to demonstrate respect for my teachers.*
> *I pledge always to demonstrate respect for every adult in my school.*
> *I pledge always to demonstrate respect for my parents.*
> *I pledge never to resort to fighting or uncontrollable arguing to solve my problems.*
> *I pledge never to use or sell drugs.*
> *I pledge never to join a gang.*
> *I pledge never to engage in criminal activity.*
> *I pledge always to strive to be the best young man that I can be.*

The experience overall was great for both my students and myself. We discussed a variety of important topics that I deemed appropriate for 4th and 5th graders. For my remaining years as a classroom teacher, I continued to engage my students in these all-male meetings once a year, usually at the beginning of the term. I continued this effort as vice principal and then principal, but now with the entire male population of the school. I began to bring in black male speakers from all walks of life. Some were professionals such as doctors, lawyers, and business people; some were blue collar workers, and others were retired. Community leaders and politicians were also always welcome to participate. I'd even bring in alumni who were currently attending college. These meetings were always powerful, provocative, and informative. My male students left these meetings feeling energized and ready to meet the challenges of the day. I was now at the point where I would conduct my young men's empowerment meetings a little more frequently. Sometimes, we'd gather together up to four times per year.

When I became a high school principal, I noticed that being a black male was becoming more and more of a challenge for many of my students as they grew older; there were simply so many distractions and temptations in the streets. I wanted to expose these students to something sustaining and meaningful, so I decided to formalize our young men's empowerment meetings by meeting with my male students once or twice a month for a minimum of two hours at a time. This way, there would be regular and ongoing reinforcement of the lessons taught in the meetings.

As a result of the ongoing success of our empowerment meetings, I determined that other schools could benefit from this approach as well. I therefore designed a comprehensive program for schools to implement, which I have been sharing with educators all over the country. Following are the components of what I have coined the Young Men's Empowerment Program:

- All-male empowerment assemblies/meetings with black male guest speakers
- All-male empowerment classroom meetings with black male guest speakers
- Small-group sessions led by black men
- One-to-one mentoring with a black male mentor
- Opportunities to meet and spend time with black male college students
- Opportunities to meet and spend time with successful black men in their work environment
- Opportunities to meet and spend time with black men in political leadership
- "Dress for Success" days
- Father-son programs
- Male retreats
- Male study groups
- Rite-of-passage programs

The first thing you will need to do is form an empowerment committee to determine what your goals for the program will be. This committee should be comprised of educators from different grade levels and a guidance counselor. It wouldn't hurt to have an administrator onboard as well. Each of the committee members must be fully committed to the empowerment program if it is going to work because the committee will essentially set the stage for the rest of the school. As an empowerment committee, you will first need to conduct a needs assessment for the male population of your school. You will need to determine what characteristics will need to change and what is currently inhibiting your young men from reaching the goals that have already been set for them. As you do this, you will also need to make an honest assessment of your school's resources and your ability to attract people with the expertise to be a part of your program.

Next, you will need to set goals for the program. Once you have determined the goals, you will need to share them with your students; they need to know why they are being asked to participate in this program, and what they are expected to take away from it. These goals should be included in "male empowerment" folders that the students will maintain and to which they will frequently refer.

A few years ago, I developed three lists composed of 150 characteristics of a man, divided into the following three categories: a man's relationship with himself, with women, and with his children. These characteristics were then converted into goals. As an example, here are the first 10 characteristics from the "man's relationship with himself" list, which could be reformatted as a handout for a meeting:

A man
1. Reads regularly; he is a life-long learner.
2. Is in life-long pursuit of his history.
3. Strives to diversify his knowledge and experiences.
4. Sets high standards and expectations for himself.
5. Is goal-oriented.
6. Sets goals and develops strategies to achieve them.
7. Aligns himself with positive, goal-oriented people.
8. Believes in his ability to achieve his goals.
9. Defines his purpose in life.
10. Is driven by his purpose.

In terms of converting these into goals, number one above written as a goal might read: "All young men in 5th grade will read 25 books of no less than 100 pages each between the first and last months of school."

Depending upon the frequency of your meetings, you should determine how many goals you should expect your males to achieve between the beginning and the end of the school year. Of course, you want to align your goals with the curriculum. The program should be assessed by the empowerment committee at the end of the semester or school year according to the goals set at the start of the process. Whatever adjustments need to be made should be made at that time.

I strongly suggest partnering with businesses and other agencies for the program, as they represent a rich source of men who can come to the school and participate in the meetings.

Although the meetings and assemblies of the program are designed for the male students, some topics would be suitable for female staff members to address, such as goal-setting, college/career planning, communication skills development, and relationship issues. For these meetings to be successful, they must have the full support of the school administration, with the goal of making them an integral part of the overall school program. If administrators do not view the empowerment meetings as relevant or meaningful, students may not do so either.

Here are some questions to consider when determining how the meetings are to be rolled out.

What Will the Meetings Look Like?

Meetings should be large-group sessions in which one or two grade levels come together to receive information in a workshop or lecture format. The location could be the auditorium, cafeteria, gymnasium, or any other room that is big enough. Presenters speak to the entire group about a variety of different issues appropriate for the grade level that pertain to the general theme of male empowerment. Presenters may wish to use multimedia resources such as slideshows and video presentations to complement their talks. Students may be required to bring notebooks and pens for note taking, and folders in which to store any handouts they may receive.

At the start of the meetings, students should be required to sit up straight. All of the adults should then introduce themselves to the students from the front of the room. Immediately following the greeting between the adults and the students, the students should be given about two or three minutes to walk around the room greeting one another with a warm hello and a handshake, then return to their seats or sit next to someone they do not know very well. The facilitator will then provide the students with an overview of the meeting.

During the meeting, students must be engaged at all times. You'll want them to have opportunities to speak and share with one another in structured activities connected to the presentation. Bear in mind that you can have more than one presenter at a meeting; this way, the students hear multiple perspectives and see that the adults are all on the same page.

At the conclusion of the meeting, students should be asked to evaluate what they have learned, both verbally and in writing. The facilitator or any of the adults can ask the students what they got out of the meeting and whether or not they thought it was worthwhile. They can also ask the students whether there was something else on the topic that they would like to have learned. If students are required to keep a journal on their thoughts about the meetings, they should be given five minutes to write their journal entries at the end of each session.

Before adjourning, it is always good to leave on a high note with pledges led either by one of the adults or by a student who is demonstrating leadership qualities and has proven that he can handle the task. Students should pledge to uphold the behaviors or values that you hope they will acquire as a result of participating in the empowerment meetings.

Following is a sample of appropriate pledges:

- I pledge to always maintain a positive attitude.
- I pledge to make sound decisions.
- I pledge to believe in myself.
- I pledge to be serious about my education.
- I pledge to be focused on achieving excellence.
- I pledge to be diligent in my efforts.
- I pledge to be disciplined in my actions.
- I pledge to be resilient after setbacks.
- I pledge to engage in independent reading every day.
- I pledge to be the best student that I can be.

These pledges are only a sample; you must develop ones that speak to the unique needs of your students. Both the leader and the students should recite the pledges with enthusiasm. Everyone in the room should be able to feel the energy. At the conclusion of the pledges, the leader will ask everyone to give each other a thunderous round of applause. At that point, the meeting will be adjourned.

Between meetings, adults should remind students who were present of what took place and of the pledges that they made. This can be done in class or one-on-one in the hallways. Bear in mind that the pledges are commitments for which the students should be held accountable.

What Do We Do If There Are Not Many Male Teachers in Our School?

If there aren't many male teachers in your school, you'll have to use the human resources that you do have available. Although it is ideal to have men speaking to your young men, the women in your school could do a fine job of bringing your young men together and speaking to them about issues that are important to their development. In such cases, the presence of men from outside the school will be especially important.

How Do We Go About Bringing Men from Outside the School into the Program?

It is always a good idea to bring in new faces with fresh perspectives to the school. Potential candidates are everywhere: every school employee and every student knows at least one man, and many men would love an invitation to come to a school and contribute toward the development of the students. It is incumbent upon the school community to seek such men out and request their assistance.

Black male students need to see and be able to talk to successful black men. We want them to see that there are men who look like them, who overcame the same challenges that the students face today by taking their education seriously and using it to their advantage.

Often, the speakers I invite to present at our empowerment meetings are concerned that the students will not be attentive and will talk or even become disrespectful. At my school, we have established that the empowerment meetings are now a part of the fabric of the school, so our students are always receptive to what we do in the meetings and are never disrespectful toward speakers. Because our students understand the overall goals and objectives of the meetings, discipline is not a concern for us at all.

It is always ideal to bring speakers back for a follow-up visit, which can help you to gauge whether or not students benefited from the presentation, as you can assess how much information students retained and how useful they feel the information is to them now. Such visits also show the students that the speakers are committed to their success. If follow-up visits are not possible, it is a good idea to discuss each speaker's presentation at the following meeting and solicit feedback from the students.

Should Grade Levels Be Combined in the Meetings?

When I was a middle school principal, I would sometimes combine all three grade levels, and sometimes I would meet with each grade level separately, depending on the goal of the meeting. At my high school, I typically will meet with each grade level separately because of the differences in maturity, interests, needs, and issues between younger and older students, but not always. Sometimes I will combine the freshmen and sophomores and the juniors and seniors; other times, I will combine seniors and freshmen and allow the seniors to conduct the meeting. In the latter formulation, the seniors can share with the freshmen their expectations of how first-year high school students should conduct themselves. Every senior who volunteers to speak is given about two minutes to convey his message to his freshman peers. It's an amazing thing to see the growth in the seniors over the years, which manifests itself in their messages to their younger "brothers." (Older and younger students can also be combined at the middle school level.)

Having said this, because of the distinct developmental differences at each grade level, my preference is to meet with each grade level separately, although time constraints may require that they be combined. Whenever I conduct grade level meetings, I find myself delivering four distinctly different messages to each grade due to the differences in needs, interests, issues, and maturity levels.

At the middle school level, the differences are very noticeable; for me, more so than at the high school level. The message to incoming 6th graders is radically different from the message for graduating 8th graders. At the 6th grade level, young men are still trying to find themselves and to adapt to their new school surroundings. At the 7th grade level, the students are at an in-between state—they are no longer new, but still a long way from graduating. At the 8th grade level, the students are thinking about high school and what it entails. Many of them are also consumed with now being the "big men on campus." At this age and grade level, they need to be exposed to messages that instruct and inspire them to become models and leaders for the younger students.

At the elementary level, the same logic applies. 3rd graders and 5th graders are in two different worlds, for example. They are not necessarily looking to hear the same thing, nor do they need to.

Of course, each school is unique, which will require that you make adjustments to your program. The bottom line is to ensure that the message matches the maturity level of the students. You want the message to be just right for the students who are in the audience.

How Frequently Should the Meetings Occur?

The frequency of the meetings will depend on a few factors, including the needs of the students and the feasibility of getting them out of class. When I started my program, I would hear complaints from staff that the meetings took time away from instruction, so the students ran the risk of falling behind. I countered these complaints with the argument that if I was successful in reaching students in this format, their change in attitude would yield changes in academic performance for the better.

Deciding on how often the meetings should occur boils down to figuring out how important your school deems the meetings to be. I recommend starting with monthly meetings, and either increasing or decreasing their frequency from there.

How Long Should the Meetings Be?

As with the frequency of the meetings, the duration of the meetings really depends on your school's own unique circumstances. You must determine how much time your students can feasibly spend out of the classroom, keeping in mind that the program should be seen as an integral part of the school culture that enhances learning for your black males.

At What Time of Day Should the Meetings Be Held?

Any time of the day should work if the students are excited to attend the meetings, but I have found that students are often fresher and more focused at the beginning of the day.

What Should Female Students Do During the Meetings?

Although my focus in this book is on black males, an empowerment program for girls is just as feasible and worthwhile as one for boys. If your school were to implement such a program, meetings for both groups of students could occur at the same time. Another option is to combine the classes of the remaining girls together while the boys are in meetings, as this will free up teachers to attend the meetings. (The same can occur for the remaining boys while the girls are in meetings.)

What About Young Male Students Who Aren't Black?

If your young male population is racially integrated, then your empowerment meetings are going to be integrated as well. This is not a problem at all. In my schools, I have found that young males of all ethnicities can benefit from empowerment programs.

What Staff Members Should Be Involved in the Meetings?

I have found that some of my strongest presenters at male empowerment meetings have been members of the custodial and security staff. Typically, they either live in or come from the same communities as the students, so they can relate to them; they understand the issues that they are dealing with and are in a good position to offer guidance and direction. Also, under normal circumstances, students don't always have opportunities to interact with custodial and security staff. The empowerment meetings offer that opportunity, allowing students to see that these staff members are "real people" just like them with real issues and problems that are similar to their own.

At my school, one of my security guards is an avid reader. Every time I see him, he has a new book. Because he reads as often as he does, he has a wealth of information in his arsenal to share with the students. He is also quite passionate about speaking with the young men and is always eager to participate in the meetings. He is truly a tremendous asset to our male empowerment program.

In addition to teachers and custodial and security personnel, the empowerment meetings are open to anyone who wants to participate. As I say to my staff all the time, even if they desire not to speak, their presence alone speaks volumes. I am pleased just to have them in the room with all of the young men.

What Topics Should Be Discussed in the Meetings?

The topics that can be discussed are endless. For example, at the middle and high school levels, I have always been comfortable engaging my male students in the following topics (among many others):

- Male/female relationships
- Fatherhood
- Peer pressure
- Friendships
- Gangs, drugs, and violence
- Community and economic development
- The importance of education and going to college
- Reading
- Goal setting
- Career planning
- Entrepreneurship
- Proper attire for different settings

What Other Components Might Be Added to the Young Men's Empowerment Program?

Here are some possible additional components to your program.

Small-Group Sessions

Small-group sessions of three to ten students have the potential of being much more personal than larger ones, as the presenters have increased opportunities to interact with students one-to-one. Students also tend to be more open and candid in more intimate settings. If your school can secure enough presenters to visit the school with some regularity, I would definitely encourage small-group sessions. Specific individuals can be assigned to specific groups of students, thus allowing relationships to develop. You may want to group students with similar issues together; for example, a group of students who exhibit similar undesirable behaviors may warrant presenters who can focus on addressing those behaviors.

One-to-One Mentoring with a Black Male Mentor

When conducting your initial needs assessment, you may determine that certain students could really benefit from a one-to-one mentor, or even just someone to listen to what is on the young man's mind. If you decide that you want to proceed with a one-to-one mentoring program, you will need to let parents and administrators know; in fact, you will probably want to have the parents of the mentees sign permission forms. One-to-one mentoring is extremely beneficial, particularly when there is an absence of men in the lives of the boys.

Opportunities to Meet and Spend Time with Black Male College Students

Black males at the elementary, middle, and high school levels need to see other black males who have had similar experiences and have now gone on to college. Your students need to see that going to college is a definite possibility if they prepare for it now—and who better to help them understand what is required than students who are presently in college? Your students will probably also relate more to college students than to adults. College students can also share with them whatever mistakes they may have made when they were the students' age, and what it took for them to overcome the mistakes. It is also a great idea for your students to actually visit a college campus and spend a day partaking of the college experience; after all, if we expect our black males to transcend their immediate surroundings, we must expose them to what lies beyond them.

Opportunities to Meet and Spend Time with Successful Black Men in Their Work Environment

This approach works particularly well when schools partner with specific companies and agencies. I can remember growing up not having a clue as to what careers really entailed. Beyond doctors and lawyers, I didn't even know what other careers there were. This lack of awareness continues to be the case with many of our young people today, particularly our black young men. So many of them do not realize that there are unlimited possibilities beyond what they see in their neighborhoods. By allowing them to visit professionals on the job, we broaden their horizons, enabling them to see a world that many of them never knew existed. Black male students should especially be made aware of black male entrepreneurs—those who decided that they did not want to work for someone else and are generating an income for themselves.

Opportunities to Meet and Spend Time with Black Men in Positions of Political Leadership

There are many black male political leaders of whom students are unaware. In addition to inviting such leaders to the school, your school should allow students to visit them in their local offices so that they can learn firsthand what political leadership encompasses. Regardless of size, many cities across the country have black male elected officials who would welcome the opportunity to partner with schools and share their experiences and expertise with your students. It's as easy as your male empowerment committee reaching out to them for an initial meeting about the goals of the program.

Dress for Success Days

In schools where uniforms are not required, students typically wear the latest styles; formal attire is usually reserved for special occasions. Over the years, in my capacity as principal, I have instituted Dress for Success days for the male population, when all of the male students are to come to school in a business suit or shirt, tie, slacks, and shoes.

I have noticed a change in students' behavior on these days: they *feel* good because they actually *look* good. They are hearing compliments about their appearance throughout the course of the day, which ultimately makes them act differently. I recommend that you institute Dress for Success days throughout the year at different intervals, based on the unique needs of the school. These days should be treated as celebrations, and staff members should make an effort to compliment each individual student throughout the day. For optimal results, take photos of the dressed-up students and post them prominently in the school lobby.

At my school, Monday is Dress for Success day—only we call it Power Monday, and it coincides with our empowerment meetings. On those days, our students are inspired both by the meetings and by the powerful message that their professional attire sends.

Father-Son Programs

I have had the opportunity of conducting a few father-son programs over the years and found them to be absolutely powerful. Fathers and sons get an opportunity to hear the same message together about their roles in relation to one another. Most of the fathers do not live in the same household as their sons; because the time they spend with their sons ranges from limited to nonexistent, father-son programs provide a good excuse to come together to engage in meaningful, quality dialogue with one another. In some cases, it gives them an opportunity to start over in their relationships. Your school, then, must endeavor to form a relationship with the fathers, particularly if they do not live in the same household as their sons. (Of course, the mother or legal guardian should be notified first and involved every step of the way.)

Male Retreats

Male retreats are another good way to bring men and your male students together for productive discussions. The retreats can take place at the school itself or somewhere else in the community, such as at a community center. The idea is to invite men of all backgrounds and walks of life to an outing where they can share their wisdom with the boys of your school. A forum such as this would be okay for parents, including mothers, to attend as well; they can observe and listen to the discussions, then engage their children in a follow-up discussion later for reinforcement. Retreats provide men with the opportunity to speak openly and honestly to the boys about life in general, and allow boys to listen to men who have already walked down the path that they are walking now. The retreats could be scheduled to occur at least four times per year.

Male Study Groups

A few years ago, a former middle school student of mine called me to inform me about a study group that he and his peers launched and called the Malcolm X Study Group. The purpose of the group was to discuss the life and legacy of Malcolm X. The students chose Malcolm X because of what he represented for black men the world over. They felt that there were many lessons to be learned through the study and analysis of his life. Each week, the young men came together to discuss a book chapter that they had assigned the previous week. They would also bring in guest speakers to further clarify points learned about Malcolm's life, legacy, and views. Study groups are a great after-school activity for students with particular interests, especially when led by a staff person who is also knowledgeable of the material to be read. Ideally, students will study black historical figures and events and engage in discussions that they may not necessarily have opportunities to engage in during normal instructional time.

How Should the Young Men's Empowerment Program Be Assessed?

At intervals throughout the school year (such as the end of each marking period), and ultimately at the end of the school year, it is imperative that the empowerment committee assess the program by comparing set goals with actual outcomes. In those areas where goals are not met, the empowerment committee will need to determine the reasons why and decide on necessary adjustments.

Conclusion

In the various motivational seminars that I conduct with black male youth, I proclaim to them that they can achieve anything in life that they want to achieve. I tell them that the only ones who can stop them from achieving their dreams are themselves. I even tell them that they can become the president of the United States if they so desire.

Over the past several years, every time I told the young men that they could become the president of the United States, I wondered if I was being honest with them. Was the United States truly ready for a black president? Teenagers would ask me if I really believed that a black man would be elected president. Then, on November 4, 2008, the world as we know it changed. Senator Barack Obama was elected the 44th president of the United States of America.

Barack Obama's election is a tremendous testament to the fact that a black male can indeed reach the highest office in the country. Your black males now have a role model who looks like them in the White House—confirmation that someone who looks like them can legitimately aspire to the highest of heights. This fact will ultimately change the way black male youth perceive themselves. They will now see that despite the stereotypes, generalizations, and negative portrayals of black men in the media, they too can aspire to heights that were in the recent past considered inconceivable. Of course, this does not imply that the challenges and obstacles of the past have disappeared; that would be a naïve notion indeed. Rather, it means that the probability for the academic success of black males increases exponentially.

When you get back into your classroom, take a look at your black male students. Take a deep look into their eyes and see the greatness in them all. The next Barack Obamas are in your classroom. Each of your black males has the potential for becoming the next president of the United States. In fact, they can become whatever it is in life that they want to become. The key to their success, however, is you. You must be able to envision them achieving greatness. You must be on a mission to make their dreams their reality. Your purpose as their teacher must be for them to maximize their potential.

The power rests in your hands. You have the power to shape your black males into the champions that they are meant to become, but you must maintain the attitude that there are no excuses on your part or theirs. You must maintain the attitude that neither failure nor mediocrity is an option in your classroom. As you stand in the front of your classroom looking into the eyes of your black male students, simply say to yourself that "the number-one determinant of the success or failure of my black male students is me," and firmly believe this.

Appendix A

50 I's for Being
a Serious Student

As a student, it is extremely important that you are successful throughout your years in school. Your grade school education is the foundation for your success. It is my hope that you will strive to achieve academic excellence in all of your classes, each and every year. If success is in fact going to be your reality, I encourage you to make the 50 *Is* below a part of your regular routine. I encourage you to review and study this list regularly, and ultimately make it a part of who you are. As you study this list, also be mindful that the key to success is to maintain an attitude that is positive and productive, and to always make wise decisions along the way. I encourage you always to be

- **Serious** about learning,
- **Focused** on achieving academic excellence,
- **Diligent** in your efforts,
- **Disciplined** in your actions, and
- **Resilient** after setbacks.

As long as you adhere to the above, while simultaneously implementing the 50 *Is* below, I am confident that the vision of academic excellence will become your permanent reality.

1. I attend school every day.
2. I arrive to school on time every day.
3. I arrive to class on time each period.
4. I consistently make the honor roll.
5. I am consistently selected "student of the month."
6. I consistently achieve academic excellence.
7. I consistently set goals and develop strategies to achieve them.

---

8. I consistently focus on my teachers, objectives and lessons—I listen, I'm attentive, I concentrate, and I participate.

9. I consistently "ace" all of my assessments.

10. I complete all homework assignments.

11. I study for a minimum of two hours every evening.

12. I read the newspaper on a daily basis.

13. I read books on a daily basis.

14. I am in constant search of new knowledge.

15. I take copious notes and ask questions when something is not clear or understood.

16. I look critically at everything I learn.

17. I strive to be accepted into a college or university.

18. I spend sufficient time in the library engaged in research and study.

19. I spend sufficient time on the Internet engaged in research and study.

20. I spend sufficient time writing to respond to, critique, or summarize what I read.

21. I am constantly preparing for my future.

22. I have a positive attitude.

23. I have high standards and expectations for myself.

24. I believe in myself and in my ability to achieve academic excellence.

25. I have a definite purpose for receiving an education.

26. I understand my obligation to excel.

27. I am determined to achieve academic excellence.

28. I have a vision for achieving academic excellence.

29. I align and surround myself with other positive, goal-oriented people.

30. I never allow someone or something to distract me from achieving excellence.

31. I never allow someone else's negativity to discourage me from achieving my goals.
32. I never accept failure as my reality.
33. I hold myself accountable for my own failure.
34. I accept obstacles as challenges to succeed.
35. I understand my responsibility as a positive role model for others.
36. I make a positive difference in my school.
37. I make a positive difference in my community.
38. I comply with all school, hallway, classroom, and cafeteria rules.
39. I consistently dress appropriately for school.
40. I exhibit the utmost respect for myself.
41. I exhibit the utmost respect for my peers.
42. I exhibit the utmost respect for my teachers.
43. I exhibit the utmost respect for every adult in my school.
44. I never bully, ridicule, or harass other students.
45. I never resort to fighting or uncontrollable arguing to solve my problems.
46. I never deface the walls of my school.
47. I never use or sell drugs.
48. I am not, nor will I ever be, a member of a gang.
49. I do not, nor will I ever, engage in criminal activity.
50. I will always make my parents and the entire school community proud of me.

Appendix B

50 I's for New and Aspiring Principals

Laypeople typically think of good principals as strong disciplinarians. I too was once guilty of thinking that in order to be an effective principal, one had to be a strong disciplinarian. However, I learned very early in my career that strong discipline didn't necessarily translate into student achievement. During my first year as a principal, I focused so much on discipline that student achievement suffered. Had I not changed my focus, my principalship would surely have been short-lived. At the start of my second year, I began to look at myself not so much as a disciplinarian, but as an instructional leader. Just as it was imperative that I see myself as the instructional leader of the building, my students and staff had to see me and feel comfortable with me in this role as well. Once I changed my behavior and began to operate as an instructional leader, my students began to achieve tremendous gains on state standardized assessments.

When I was interviewing for my first administrative position as a vice principal, a superintendent told me that he was looking for a strong instructional leader. He said to me that anyone can be a disciplinarian, but effective principals led their schools instructionally. His words have remained with me throughout my career. As a new or aspiring principal, you too must first and foremost see yourself as the lead educator of your school. You must therefore come to the realization that the overall academic progress of your school is directly tied to how well you lead your school.

Following is a list of affirmations for principals who aspire to see themselves as instructional leaders. To effectively leading your

---

Note: All material in this appendix is copyright © 2006 by Baruti K. Kafele and can also be found on his Web site, http://www.principalkafele.com.

school instructionally, I recommend that you read, study, internalize, and implement these affirmations regularly from the outset of your career.

1. I am the instructional leader of my school.
2. I see myself as the number-one determinant of the success or failure of my students.
3. I understand that, as the instructional leader of my school, my priority must be on student achievement and improvement in instruction.
4. I am very knowledgeable of my district curriculum, state content standards, and state assessment specifications.
5. I hold my staff accountable for the implementation of the district curriculum and state content standards.
6. I set the tone for my school at the start of every day through positive, motivating, and uplifting morning announcements.
7. I consistently strive to keep my staff and students motivated and excited about learning.
8. I praise my students and staff for their accomplishments, both privately and publicly.
9. I spend the majority of my time each day in classrooms observing instruction and learning.
10. I provide immediate feedback to my staff after observing their instruction.
11. I have a definite *purpose* for leading that drives everything I say and everything I do.
12. I treat my instructional leadership not as a job, profession, or career, but as a *mission*.
13. I am on a personal mission to ensure that all of my students achieve academic excellence.

14. I have a short-range and long-range personal vision of what I expect my students to achieve.

15. I regularly communicate my personal mission and vision to my students and staff.

16. I engage my staff in the development of the school mission and vision statements.

17. I ensure that my students and staff can articulate the school mission and vision statements.

18. I have high academic standards and expectations for my students and staff, and I believe that they will attain them.

19. I regularly communicate my high academic standards and expectations to my students and staff.

20. I hold my teachers accountable for ensuring that all of my students achieve academic excellence, which includes meeting or exceeding district, state, and federally-mandated benchmarks.

21. I model what I expect of my students and staff.

22. I conduct daily self-reflections and self-assessments of my instructional leadership.

23. I maintain a collegial relationship with my staff.

24. I ensure that my new teachers are paired with competent veteran teachers.

25. I encourage my veteran teachers to observe the instruction of my new teachers, and vice versa.

26. I provide my new teachers with maximum support and ongoing professional development.

27. I participate in staff team meetings and provide input and leadership where warranted.

28. I regularly collaborate with my staff regarding instruction.

29. I use staff meeting time for staff professional development.

30. I engage all staff during professional development meetings.
31. I regularly provide professional literature to my staff.
32. I adhere to my own written plan of action for student achievement daily.
33. I am well-organized in my daily routine of observing instruction and learning.
34. I use data to drive all instructional decisions.
35. I strive to empower my staff by involving them in school-level planning and decision making.
36. I ensure that instruction in my classrooms is student-centered.
37. I ensure that my staff uses a variety of instructional approaches and strategies in an effort to address the different learning styles and needs of all of my students.
38. I ensure that my staff maximizes student time on task.
39. I ensure that my school and classrooms are clean and well-maintained, and that the school and classroom climate and culture are conducive to learning.
40. I have developed extended day opportunities for those students who are struggling academically.
41. I demonstrate an appreciation and respect for my students and staff.
42. I refuse to accept failure in my school.
43. I refuse to make excuses for any failure my students may experience.
44. I accept responsibility and will be held accountable for student success and failure.
45. I base my beliefs about how children learn upon my own research and experiences.
46. I read professional development literature on the latest research in instructional leadership.

47. I attend professional development conferences and work-shops addressing instructional leadership.
48. I confer with colleagues and other educational leaders with an eye toward my development as an instructional leader.
49. I belong to professional organizations.
50. I make parental and community engagement a priority in my practice as an instructional leader.

Appendix C

50 I's for
Effective Teaching

As a classroom teacher, you have chosen the most important of all professions. You have chosen to take on the responsibility of preparing young people for future success. I developed the following list of affirmations in an effort to increase the probability that you meet the criteria for mastery in teaching. If you review, internalize, and implement these affirmations on a regular basis, the probability for student success will increase exponentially.

1. I know, appreciate, and respect the history and culture of my students.
2. I have a culturally responsive approach to instruction.
3. I have a definite purpose for teaching.
4. I treat teaching not as a job, profession, or career, but as a mission.
5. I have a vision for what I expect my students to achieve.
6. I see myself as the number-one determinant of the success or failure of my students.
7. I see myself as a role model, and therefore always conduct myself professionally.
8. I conduct daily self-reflections and self-assessments.
9. I strive to motivate, educate, and empower my students daily.
10. I have high expectations and standards for all of my students and believe that they will reach them.
11. I instill in my students a sense of purpose for their education daily.
12. I hold my students accountable for setting academic goals and developing strategies for achieving them.

13. I consistently teach with energy, enthusiasm, passion, and optimism.
14. I have an unequivocal commitment to my students' academic growth and development.
15. I am an expert in the content areas I teach.
16. I have a student-centered approach to instruction.
17. I differentiate my instruction based upon the different learning styles and ability levels of my students.
18. I use a variety of instructional approaches for the benefit of my students.
19. I have an interdisciplinary approach to instruction.
20. I regularly incorporate technology into my instruction.
21. I am knowledgeable of brain theory and how the brain processes information.
22. I am knowledgeable of child development theory.
23. I plan systematically for each day, week, month, and school year.
24. I regularly use achievement data to develop my lessons.
25. I am highly organized.
26. I maintain a classroom environment that is conducive to learning.
27. I am a superb classroom manager.
28. I love, appreciate, and respect my students.
29. I appreciate and respect the communities in which my students reside.
30. I do not fear my students, their parents, or the communities in which they reside.
31. I treat all of my students equally and fairly.
32. I know about all of my students' lives beyond academics.
33. I attend student functions beyond the ones I organize.
34. I eat lunch with my students.

35. I teach students, not subjects.
36. I make learning fun, stimulating, and engaging.
37. I teach and encourage critical thinking regularly.
38. I refuse to allow failure to occur in my classroom.
39. I refuse to make excuses for any failure my students may experience.
40. I accept responsibility and accountability for student success and failure.
41. I do not use the race and socioeconomic status of my students as an excuse for their performance.
42. I am a lifelong learner, always striving to become a better teacher.
43. I participate in ongoing professional development.
44. I have a collegial relationship with my colleagues.
45. I accept constructive feedback from my colleagues and administrators.
46. I act upon suggestions from my colleagues and administrators for improvement.
47. I see myself as an integral part of a team, not an island by myself.
48. I maximize parental involvement by developing strong bonds with all of my students' parents.
49. I notify parents of both problems and successes.
50. I visit the homes of my students.

BIBLIOGRAPHY

Asante, M. K. (1988). *Afrocentricity*. Trenton, NJ: Africa World Press.

Bennett, L., Jr. (1982). *Before the Mayflower: A history of Black America*. Chicago: Johnson Publishing Co.

Burt, M., Jr. (1969). *Black inventors of America*. Portland, OR: National Book Company.

Davis, D. (2005). *A crisis action plan*. East Orange, NJ: B-Cap Press.

Delpit, L. (2006). *Other people's children: Cultural conflict in the classroom*. New York: The New Press.

Fashola, S. (2005). *Educating African American males*. Thousand Oaks, CA: Corwin Press.

Franklin, J. H. (2000). *From slavery to freedom*. New York: Random House.

Gay, G. (2000). *Culturally responsive teaching*. New York: Teachers College Press.

Hale, J. E. (1982). *Black children: Their roots, culture and learning styles*. Baltimore: The Johns Hopkins University Press.

Haley, A. (1964). *The autobiography of Malcolm X: As told to Alex Haley*. New York: Ballantine Books.

Hill, P. (1992). *Coming of age: African American male rites of passage*. Chicago: African American Images.

Hilliard, A. G., Payton-Stewart, L., & Williams, L. O. (1990). *Infusion of African and African American content in the school curriculum*. Morristown, NJ: Aaron Press.

Hopkins, R. (1997). *Educating black males: Critical lessons in schooling, community and power*. New York: State University of New York Press.

Howard, G. R. (2006). *We can't teach what we don't know: White teachers, multiracial schools.* New York: Teachers College Press.

Hrabowski, F. A., Maton, K. I., & Grief, G. L. (1998). *Beating the odds: Raising academically successful African American males.* New York: Oxford University Press.

Jackson, J. (1970). *Introduction to African civilizations.* Secaucus, NJ: The Citadel Press.

Kafele, B. K. (2004). *A Handbook for teachers of African American children.* Jersey City, NJ: Baruti Publishing.

Kunjufu, J. (1985). *Countering the conspiracy to destroy black boys* (Vol. I). Chicago: African American Images.

Kunjufu, J. (1988*). To be popular or smart: The black peer group.* Chicago: African American Images.

Kunjufu, J. (2002). *Black students, middle class teachers.* Chicago: African American Images.

Ladson-Billings, G. (1994). *The Dreamkeepers: Successful teachers of African American children.* San Francisco: Jossey-Bass.

Madhubuti, H. R. (1990). *Black men: Single, dangerous, obsolete?* Chicago: Third World Press.

McKinnon, J. D., & Bennett, C. E. (2005). *We the people: Blacks in the United States (Census 2000 Special Reports).* Retrieved January 25, 2009, from http://www.census.gov/prod/2005pubs/censr-25.pdf

Noguera, P. (2008). *The trouble with black boys.* San Francisco: Jossey-Bass.

Parker, K. (2008, June 18). Calling all fathers—and mothers, too. *The Washington Post.* Retrieved January 25, 2009, from http://www.postwriters group.com/archives/park080618.htm

Perkins, U. E. (2005). *Harvesting new generations: The positive development of black youth.* Chicago: Third World Press.

Schott Foundation for Public Education. (2008). *Given half a chance: The Schott 50-state report on public education and black males.* Retrieved January 24, 2009, from http://www.blackboysreport.org

Shabazz, B. (1970). *Malcolm X on Afro American history.* New York: Pathfinder Press.

Tatum, A. (2005). *Teaching reading to black adolescent males.* Portland, ME: Stenhouse Publishers.

Van Sertima, I. (1986). *Blacks in science: Ancient and modern.* New Brunswick, NJ: Transaction Books.

Van Sertima, I. (1989). *Nile Valley civilizations.* New Brunswick, NJ: Transaction Books.

Wilson A. (1991). *Awakening the natural genius of black children.* New York: Afrikan World Info Systems.

Winbush, R. (2001). *The warrior method.* New York: Amistad.

Woodson, C. G. (1933). *The miseducation of the Negro.* Washington, DC: The Associated Publishers.

Zaslavsky, C. (1979). *Africa counts: Number and pattern in African culture.* Westport, CT: Lawrence & Hill Company.

ABOUT
THE AUTHOR

Award-winning educator Baruti K. Kafele has
excelled as both teacher and principal for 20 years.
As a classroom teacher of students in grades 4–8 in
East Orange, New Jersey, he was selected as Teacher
of the Year in both the East Orange School District
and Essex County Public Schools. He was also
selected for inclusion in *Who's Who Among America's Teachers* six times.
As a principal, Kafele led the transformation of three different middle
schools and one high school. His work at Sojourner Truth Middle
School in East Orange helped to transform it into one of the highest
performing urban middle schools in the entire state of New Jersey.

Kafele is currently the principal of Newark Tech High School in
Newark, New Jersey, which is recognized by *U.S. News and World
Report* as one of the best high schools in the nation. He is also a
national educational consultant, motivational speaker, and author
of the bestselling books *A Black Parent's Handbook to Educating Your
Children* (*Outside of the Classroom*) (1994) and *A Handbook for Teachers
of African American Children* (2004).

Kafele can be reached via his Web site, http://www.principalkafele.com.